I
Blessed
You
With
Cancer

Jauen Eischeid
John 3:30

Chelsea Eischeid
Romans 15:13

I
Blessed
You
With
Cancer

KAREN *and* CHELSEA EISCHEID

TATE PUBLISHING
AND ENTERPRISES, LLC

Published by Tate Publishing & Enterprises, LLC
127 E. Trade Center Terrace | Mustang, Oklahoma 73064 USA
1.888.361.9473 | www.tatepublishing.com

Tate Publishing is committed to excellence in the publishing industry. The company reflects the philosophy established by the founders, based on Psalm 68:11,
"The Lord gave the word and great was the company of those who published it."

Book design copyright © 2013 by Tate Publishing, LLC. All rights reserved.
Cover design by Rodrigo Adolfo
Interior design by Mary Jean Archival

Published in the United States of America

ISBN: 978-1-62510-740-4
1. Religion / Christian Life / Death, Grief, Bereavement
2. Religion / Christian Life / Family
12.12.13

Dedication

The Divine Mercy

Acknowledgements

A sincere "thank you" to all whom in anyway encouraged and inspired this book to be what it is. *What it is* and where it is going, God knows the plans. We have only to *trust* and to *let God*.

Chelsea, Jake, Zach and my Paul, I humbly thank you for showering me with who you sincerely are and the love which is firmly planted in your hearts and souls. Through anxiety and uncertainty we clung together, as a family. God truly blesses each one of us in unique ways.

I love you more!

Introduction

Track meets somewhat compare to our cancer journey. God's "gift" flung us unprepared into "starting blocks" for countless sprinting events. We hadn't grasped the technique of getting in or up and out of them.

The low hurdles appeared unbelievably high. Our family was inexperienced in trying to leap over them with style and grace before hitting one, then falling face first onto the blacktop.

Running in the outside lanes presents a false sense of achievement. It is impossible to grasp the whole outcome of the race except for the lone runner striving right beside you.

"Ready…set…," did not transpire. The sound of the gun went off without any acknowledged warning.

Paul, the kids, and I endured unremitting winds, icy rains, freezing snow, and blistering heat. Each new event gave us hope to possibly scratch, place, or win, but we soon encountered disappointment and defeat.

In our race with time, dealing with cancer became the pulled hamstrings, knee injuries, sprains, shin splints, heat exhaustion, and many other frustrations and setbacks in life. Every event drained us of energy and spirit. After numerous times of falling and failing, it remained important that we pull one another up off the rough asphalt to "*press on*" with the race and with life. We witnessed weakness and exhaustion as we drew closer to the final laps. We couldn't finish alone.

The "bell" hailing the last lap on the relay never rang. The passing of the baton remained steady and silent as did the days and weeks. Every so often we heard from the sidelines, "long strides" or "pick up the pace." An occasional frustration of dropping the baton or going out of our assigned lane didn't disqualify us. The lost meet continued. As a team or contending alone, our family struggled to prevail.

With persistence, we kept our eyes on the finish line, the string, the tape, the end of the race. *God.*

> Do you not know that the runners in the stadium all run in the race, but only one wins the prize? Run so as to win.
>
> 1 Corinthians 9:24

> I have competed well; I have finished the race; I have kept the faith.
>
> 2 Timothy 4:7

Fragments of our life events are being kept confidential for my family's sake of privacy. Some of our stories are not meant to be shared at this time. I truly respect the requests of my children. If and when my children desire to share with the world, they are welcome to write their own personal narratives.

These stories, most likely will differ from yours, but in visiting with friends, I find several of their stories quite similar. Many of us possess in ourselves a beautiful life lesson worth sharing with others.

After making the daunting decision to write this book, I couldn't recognize where my starting point should be. Sitting down in front of our computer, doubt and skepticism ravaged my thoughts. I stared sheepishly at the keyboard for a period of time. A "mustard seed" of courage initiated my first paragraph.

I began typing one small insignificant sentence, a sentence as if written by my daughter while in kindergarten or first grade. This sentence was minimal, but God intervened. The Holy Spirit became the frontrunner in my improbable effort and guided me through each thought and in every word. Realization, awareness, and appreciation developed with my inspirations. I perceived new insights of what defines genuine compassion.

During the first bout with Renal Cell cancer, our first grade daughter, Chelsea, transpired as daddy's little angel, the sparkle in Paul's eyes.

Jake, our first born son, was only five years old. Paul frequently saw glimpses of "himself" in Jake.

Zach, our youngest, was Paul's "personal touch from Heaven." Tears once again streamed down his cheeks when he saw the birth of our third child, a second son.

Chels, Jake, Zach, and I partook in significant roles in the completion of Paul's circle in life, his desire to receive love and to give love.

God decided he wasn't ready for Paul to be with him our first jolt, when cancer shattered our lives. He graced our family with precious time, a gift often taken for granted. Hopefully, we used this blessing with wisdom, creating countless new treasured memories, taking less for granted, and loving one another abundantly more than we previously had.

We made time for family vacations. Jake and Zach learned how to catch a baseball before getting hit in the nose by a fast ball and ride a bike without training wheels. Picnics on a blanket spread out in the middle of our living room carpet were Chelsea's favorite meal time with the family. Chelsea laughing alongside her dad, after seeing me fall face first into the cattle yard muck created amusing memories we still laugh about today. He granted us extra years of planting and of harvesting. Time needed to be used wisely, to show love, to receive love, and to get our affairs in order.

We prayed together and enjoyed family meals together. Paul and I watched silly theatrical skits performed by all three of the kids in our parlor. Paul piled up humongous snow piles after blizzards. Wintery memories of icy snow being transported from their boots to my front porch still make us smile.

During the second round of cancer, I questioned Paul if it would bother him if we made early funeral arrangements. This didn't bother him at all. Chelsea, Zach, and I picked out an oak coffin for Paul. Jake decided not to help, and I understood. Paul thought the casket in the picture was beautiful.

You may think this is grotesque, but it's an important event. I wanted Paul to be a part of the decisions for his own funeral. The healing process needed to begin at some point.

Paul became involved. He chose his pallbears, his suit, and his tie. Chelsea chose songs and photographs her dad favored so that our funeral director Tony Levander could make the slide show come alive! Thank you, Tony!

But, like every normal family, disputes existed. We rapidly concluded that arguments were an extensive waste of time and energy just to prove one point of view over another. The clock kept ticking. We didn't have to prove anything but love while we could.

My wish is these words will help others deal with the loss of a loved one, learn what genuine compassion entails, increase personal spiritual growth, and intensify the need for God's Ocean of Mercy and his burning love for each and every soul. No matter how immoral, corrupt, insignificant, and little we see ourselves as, God eternally forgives. His Ocean of Mercy is infinite and everlasting.

With his holy gaze from the cross, *you* are the one he notices before everyone else. With sublime love, he waits for you. He desires your thirst for *Him*!

I disclosed several of my stories to close friends, each one departing with different stances. Other friends left with eyes filled with tears of hope and belief, while some walked away with empty looks of disbelief. They didn't have confidence in what I revealed, but I respect their convictions. These stories are not meant to persuade or sway beliefs or values in any way or form.

My only desire is to share with you our journey of experiences and to allow us the blessed privilege to remember, to laugh, to cry, and to allow the ultimate joy of healing. Hopefully, these chapters express how each one of us is thoroughly blessed in ordinary events. We must unlock our hearts. Then, our eyes will be opened, and we will be capable of absolutely trusting in Him.

I am not an expert in the laws and decrees of my Catholic religion. With my modest upbringing, my knowledge consists of basic information and simple prayers. My children unknowingly increased my understandings of the Catholic religion as their grade levels advanced at our Catholic schools. The blessing of this knowledge is priceless. I express gratitude to my late husband Paul for persevering in his religious upbringing, his courage, and his faith. We possessed a stack of unpaid bills and no money. Yet, he seriously stated to me "our kids are getting a Catholic education. Period."

> Teach us to count our days aright, that we may gain wisdom of heart.
>
> Psalm 90:12

> He said to them, "Because of your little faith. Amen, I say to you, if you have faith the size of a mustard seed, you will say to this mountain, 'Move from here to there,' and it will move." Nothing will be impossible for you."
>
> Matthew 17:20

Journal One

Chapter 1

*3*_11! 311! I know how to do this! 311! What is wrong with this phone?_ Eventually, my thirteen-year-old daughter's trembling fingers dialed the correct numbers: 9-1-1.

Less than fifty yards away, her daddy lay on the cold, hard cement slab outside the old garage. Unaware of actual happenings, Chelsea spoke to the rescue unit operator explaining, "I think my dad is having a stroke!"

Without delay, Chelsea disclosed directions to our family farm. She quickly joined her two younger brothers and me in viewing a sight we never thought possible. A typical Sunday morning began turning our lives into a continuous tail spin further than hell and back.

At 8:15 I laid in bed, thinking how farm life graced us with peace and yet how life was unchanging as the warm sun streamed through the window. Chelsea, Jake, and Zach camped out in our front yard the night before.

My husband of fifteen years, Paul, planned on driving out to the family's west pasture to check on the herd of cattle belonging to him and his cousins, Red and Bill Eischeid. One of our Sunday family traditions we took for granted was about to be altered.

Paul checked the back of his white '97 Ford pickup for items he might have needed. He found an aged hammer, wire cutter and stretcher, assortment of tarnished nails stored inside a rusty paint can, pieces of loose barbed wire, and several new wooden posts. A couple gallons of gas for the water pump and several salt blocks and bags of mineral for the cattle were arranged in the bed of the Ford. Prepared to demolish persistent musthistles, a sharp corn knife embellished with gray duct tape wrapped around its handle lay hidden under the back seat of the pickup.

There was one more significant thing to accomplish. Paul felt it essential to check who was accompanying him on this Sunday's adventure.

A "trip to the pasture" consisted of excitement and suspense. A challenging game of "Who Can Spot the Cow First?" commenced once the truck tires hit the soft sandy ground. Everyone was on the lookout for a black speck on the prairie horizon.

The kids swelled with both fear and excitement as they jumped feet-first off the lip of the sand cliff and then experienced their toes squish into the warm, moist sand below. They happily tumbled and rolled into the depths and mystery of the prairie blowout.

We embraced every second as Dad drove up and over the edge of the hills, with nothing visible except for the blue sky. The uneven ground resulted in us bobbing up and down on our journey. Before heading home, we enjoyed exploring countless old cow trails lined for miles with dazzling blissful sunflowers.

We were in no hurry traveling down the low maintenance country roads, comparing farm crops, hitting every achievable mud puddle, and listening to his oldies stations. This was our heaven.

Just Daddy and you, nothing made the heart swell more. The entertaining excursion concluded with a cold Dr. Pepper or a quick melting ice cream cone from the local gas station. Our lives were simple, but yet so perfect.

It didn't happen! After experiencing an adventure in the front yard overnight, Jake and Zach decided on playing basketball in the early morning. They also were enjoying a challenge of pitching a soccer ball toward several untiring barn swallows which dived at the boys, thinking they could hit and knock one down.

"Dad, what's the smartest animal?"

"I am," Paul joked with Zach as he started falling to the cement.

"Ahh, I'm having a stroke!"

These words got Jake's full attention; he glanced over in the direction of his dad. Paul faced a difficult time standing as he clutched both of his numb legs.

Ignoring a slight numbness in one leg several times the past week, Paul thought nothing of it and kept his mind on more important things: baseball! Hindsight is always so obvious.

"I need your mom, go get Mom!" Paul told the boys as he collapsed into a realm of no sensation: hearing or remembering.

The minimal time frame in waiting seemed like an eternity in ten-year-old Zach's eyes as he observed his daddy's strange behavior. To escape this dreamlike reality, he decided to flee into the house to find out why his brother was taking so long with getting their mom.

Not wanting to return to his dad's side with the rest of us, Zach rushed to his upstairs bedroom. He clutched the recent baseball medal he won with "coach dad" and prayed to God.

With persistent, unbearable headaches exploding behind my right eye and forehead for several weeks, explorative surgery became the lone option. Two days earlier this surgical procedure caused both eyes to swell shut. The night before Paul's fateful morning a diminishing of swelling enabled me to gaze through small slits. I gave the impression I had participated in a big scuffle. I remembered the EMTs glancing at me with questioning eyes.

Chelsea and Jake flew into the bedroom,

"Dad needs you! I think he's having a stroke!"

I found Paul lying flat on the brutal cement. While his body shook hard, his face turned purple and his lips became a bluish color. His eyes rolled back in their sockets. After a loud scream from me, Chelsea ran into the house to phone for assistance. Chelsea's intuition came true; she would be the one to call for help. The many times I practiced with my kids when they were younger paid off. The four of us overflowed with terror, trembling, and tears.

Years later, as I sorted through dusty shoe boxes filled with school papers and writing projects, I discovered one paper clarifying a small fraction of how ten-year-old Zach perceived "*the day*":

"Ya know, life was great, until *the day*. That day was so bad, I would've been down "farther" than the dumps."

After retrieving Zach, we all knelt down beside Paul on the hard gritty cement. The loose gravel burrowed deep into our bare knees as we individually told Paul how much we loved him. Their dad's behavior was viewed as bizarre and having to kneel next to him seemed eerie.

The minimal time frame awaiting the rescue squad dragged like an eternity to us. Only three miles from town, what took them so long?

Skip, our rat terrier, sensed something out of the ordinary. We struggled to keep him from lying down beside Paul. Each time we moved him, he crouched down low and crawled back to Paul's side. Restraining Skip from entering the ambulance seemed like a futile challenge.

One of the boys sprinted into the house to retrieve a pillow to place under their dad's head to ease him of any discomfort from the cement. Our voices and bodies quivered while we prayed.

The *Chaplet of Divine Mercy* grounded us the next several months. It became our raft on which we clung. The future submerged as our ambitions and dreams sunk into a deep abyss of hopelessness.

The Chaplet of The Divine Mercy

How to Recite the Chaplet

The Chaplet of Mercy is recited using ordinary rosary beads of five decades. The Chaplet is preceded by two opening prayers from the Diary of Saint Faustina and followed by a closing prayer.

1. Make the Sign of the Cross
    In the name of the Father, and of the Son, and of the Holy Spirit. Amen.

2. Optional Opening Prayers
    You expired, Jesus, but the source of life gushed forth for souls, and the ocean of mercy opened up for the whole world. O Fount of Life, unfathomable Divine Mercy, envelop the whole world and empty Yourself out upon us.

    O Blood and Water, which gushed forth from the Heart of Jesus as a fountain of Mercy for us, I trust in You!

3. Our Father
    Our Father, Who art in heaven, hallowed be Thy name; Thy kingdom come; Thy will be done on earth as it is in heaven. Give us this day our daily bread; and forgive us our trespasses as we forgive those who trespass against us; and lead us not into temptation, but deliver us from evil, Amen.

4. Hail Mary
    Hail Mary, full of grace. The Lord is with thee. Blessed art thou amongst women, and blessed is the fruit of thy womb, Jesus. Holy

Mary, Mother of God, pray for us sinners, now and at the hour of our death, Amen.

5. The Apostle's Creed

I believe in God, the Father almighty, Creator of heaven and earth, and in Jesus Christ, His only Son, our Lord, who was conceived by the Holy Spirit, born of the Virgin Mary, suffered under Pontius Pilate, was crucified, died and was buried; He descended into hell; on the third day He rose again from the dead; He ascended into heaven, and is seated at the right hand of God the Father almighty; from there He will come to judge the living and the dead. I believe in the Holy Spirit, the holy Catholic Church, the communion of saints, the forgiveness of sins, the resurrection of the body, and life everlasting. Amen.

6. The Eternal Father

Eternal Father, I offer you the Body and Blood, Soul and Divinity of Your Dearly Beloved Son, Our Lord, Jesus Christ, in atonement for our sins and those of the whole world.

7. On the Ten Small Beads of Each Decade

For the sake of His sorrowful Passion, have mercy on us and on the whole world.

8. Repeat for the remaining decades

Saying the "Eternal Father" on the "Our Father" bead and then ten "For the sake of His sorrowful Passion" on the following "Hail Mary" beads.

9. Conclude with Holy God (Repeat three times)
   Holy God, Holy Mighty One, Holy Immortal One, have mercy on us and on the whole world.

10. Optional Closing Prayer
    Eternal God, in whom mercy is endless and the treasury of compassion — inexhaustible, look kindly upon us and increase Your mercy in us, that in difficult moments we might not despair nor become despondent, but with great confidence submit ourselves to Your holy will, which is Love and Mercy itself.
    marian.org

Rejoice in hope, endure in affliction, persevere in prayer.

Romans 12:12

Chapter 2

Within the hour, we received distressing information that Paul experienced a Grand Mal seizure. X-rays revealed cancer spots on his brain and lungs. What we assumed would never be a threat to us again escalated back into our lives, taunting us.

Seven years earlier on November 13th, 2000, Paul was diagnosed with Renal Cell kidney cancer. His odds of surviving were low. Blood in the urine appeared to be the initial symptom, but we weren't too concerned, thinking the major problem was a urinary tract infection.

Minutes before leaving for his first appointment, Paul felt a hard area by his kidneys. While questioning what it could possibly be, both Paul and I let this vital clue slide out of our minds as we focused only on the urine problem. He must not have mentioned the firm area during his scheduled time. With Paul's doctor appointment completed and with no avail with antibiotics, he was referred to a cancer specialist in Norfolk, Nebraska.

Stomach flu infiltrated our house the evening before and left me home with our kids so Paul went to the appointment alone. My initial thought of having children up during the night with the flu was draining. After reflecting back in the time of our family's experiences with cancer, that "little bug" isn't so big and

KAREN AND CHELSEA EISCHEID

bad. There are "bigger bugs!" A small amount of "throw up" now seemed like a minor cross.

With spiritual strength, Paul's faith remained unyielding throughout his entire journey. I questioned, disliked, and found fault and arguments against God's will.

With his patience, his perpetual love, and with time, I discovered I needed to keep my mind, eyes, and heart focused on *him*. God would guide our family through this hell. With reluctance, I unwillingly let him have absolute control. I allowed him to shepherd us. In our daily human frustrations, failures, and skepticism he patiently taught us trust. "Jesus, I Trust In You!"

In the *"Diary: Divine Mercy in My Soul"* by Maria Faustina Kowalska, Jesus said to Sister Faustina;

> … I am Love and Mercy itself. When a soul approaches Me with trust, I fill it with such an abundance of graces that it cannot contain them within itself, but radiates them to other souls (1074).
>
> …I have opened My Heart as a living fountain of mercy. Let all souls draw life from it. Let them approach this sea of mercy with great trust (Diary, 1520). On the cross, the fountain of My mercy was opened wide by the lance for all souls — no one have I excluded! (1182). I am offering people a vessel with which they are to keep coming for graces to the fountain of mercy. That vessel is this image with the signature: "Jesus, I trust in You" (327). The graces of My mercy are drawn by means of one

vessel only, and that is — trust. The more a soul trusts, the more it will receive (1578).

I often wonder about Paul's reactions to the shocking news of his first bout with cancer. The guilt torments me. Where was my support for him on one of his darkest days?

Pale and emotionless, he stood in the porch with bags of food in his arms. How did he have the courage to shop for groceries after hearing his death sentence? With desolate eyes and the statement mentally implanted, Paul told me, "I have cancer."

Shocked and stunned by the words coming from his calm voice, I embraced Paul. I prayed that a miracle would banish this newcomer from our life.

An early morning nephrectomy two days later detached the encapsulated cancer and right kidney. The surgeon asked me if I wanted to view the cancer mass. With a quick glimpse of this five pound manifestation; I noticed its resemblance of a pot roast. Chemo and radiation weren't required. The attending surgeons believed they removed the entirety of the incurable cells.

Paul's final pathology diagnosis following surgery blessed our family with a small flicker of hope: five lymph nodes, one perirenal lymph node, the ureter, and the adrenal gland were negative for malignancy. The Gross evaluation showed a renal cell carcinoma that replaces approximately 80% of the kidney. The tumor did not invade through the renal capsule. There was a tumor present in the renal vein with the distal vein margin negative for malignancy.

Doctors informed our family with five cancer-free years, Paul would be lucky. Paul should be quite fortunate after seven years elapsed. At every six month checkup, Paul received a clean bill of health. We unintentionally let our guards down with each examination that passed.

An exam in January of 2007 confirmed a seventh year of being cancer-free. Yet, only six months later with the help of a seizure, malignant cells in his brain, lymph nodes, several ribs, hip bone, and both lungs were detected. The dormant cells blossomed.

In recalling earlier memories of cancer free checkups, I noticed Paul's weight loss and him walking with a limp. Together we rationalized his sore lower back resulted from him pitching and hitting too many balls at the Pee-Wee baseball practices; cancer never entered the picture or our conversation. A friend even asked me at one of the evening ball games about whether Paul hurt his back or leg. Cancer consumed his pelvis bone throughout the entire baseball season.

A quiet morning turned into a full blown nightmare. I thank God for one of many blessings—family! For the weekend, my baby sister Terri Ann (Tootsie) was on a brief visit at our parents' farm, northeast of Neligh. A higher power placed her where she needed to be that morning.

It was crucial that the youngest of my ten siblings transformed into our G.P.S. The four of us followed her back to Omaha, the setting of the hospital where Paul was being transported by ambulance.

Compassionately, Tootsie shared her residence with us the next two weeks. With her living minutes from the health center, she became our taxi driver and our strength. She fed us, worked hard to preserve our positive morale, and kept the rest of our family updated. Persistently, she sheltered Chels, Jake, and Zach's emotional state with 4th of July fireworks, eating out, and the zoo, instead of them contemplating on their dad.

Unpleasant thoughts lingered as unstable ideas spun violently in my mind. I pictured myself becoming a widow, our children fatherless, and the fears of immortality Paul faced. Could I raise these kids without a father?

Countless anxiety attacks confronted me during the night hours and throughout the days. Upon waking each morning, I experienced a quiet peace, but within seconds reality set in and so did the angst.

This second round of cancer rolled into our lives with rage and fury. Inconsolable tears fell after the results of the first tests. God graced our family with a specific gift from him, *but we didn't want it*. Paul faced his mortality with fear and anxiety. Waiting in the hospital room left Paul's red eyes overflowing with tears trickling down his terrified face.

"I'm not ready to leave you and the kids yet. I don't want to die. The kids need a dad!"

Having warnings signs of a severe headache, I had my blood pressure taken. Not surprised of its results, my brain sensed a damaging explosion.

The family spent two weeks in Omaha and the Nebraska Medical Center. Excessive time consisted of waiting for an array of tests to be conducted and a never-ending line of doctors, each a dedicated expert in his field of anatomy and cancer. We patiently awaited numerous results. One specific test scheduled for 8:00 a.m. eventually transpired later the following day. In questioning the nurse on duty, she educated us, "gunshot victims have main priority." This statement left me thinking of our family's survival. My animal instincts quietly contemplated, *"My husband is dying. Where is his priority?"*

Resuming to "normal" and forgetting this nightmare became our deepest desire. What happened to a once peaceful Sunday morning with the warm sun streaming through the bedroom window?

Chelsea and Jake received a ride home early with some friends who were in Omaha and heading back to Elgin. A diehard in the baseball world, Jake didn't want to miss any of his games. The Steve and Becky Kerkman family invited them to be overnights guest for as long as need be. Mentally unprepared to be away from his mom *or his dad*, Zach decided to stay the remainder of the Omaha trip.

After the first day and the initial shock, Paul went into denial. He portrayed himself as happy, healthy and positive constantly. Each doctor seemed to give Paul the false hope and impression of being cured. I saw the situation differently. For example, Paul's lungs were so spotted with cancer. The individual spots grew into a mass impossible to count, and the cells metastasized all through Paul's body.

I didn't represent a humble Christian. I burst Paul's bubble because it was hard watching him act like his cancer was curable. I enquired if he understood he would die soon. He admitted he knew.

Paul began to prepare himself for human misery, spiritual readiness, and an unbelievable agonizing end to his existence. He still kept a positive attitude toward life, God, and miserable me! All five of us returned home. With the help of Becky Kerkman, Chelsea and Jake fashioned a banner reading, "Welcome Home, Dad!" above the parlor doors. We were so glad to have everyone back together in the farm house.

Yet, we sensed a sixth, a stranger moved into our home. Our lives centered on this hideous outsider. This visitor refused to leave without taking something of significant value with him when he left: Paul.

As we sat quietly in our pew at the end of Mass one Sunday, I glanced over at Paul and our three kids.

"Father, please bless my family."

Out of the silence, I heard, *"I blessed you with cancer."*

> Behold, I know your thoughts, and the arguments you rehearse against me.
>
> Job 21:27

31

Chapter 3

I lay on the couch, wrapped head to toe in a heavy, fleece blanket and inches from Paul's rented hospital bed. One room in our house transformed into a private sickbay. Instead of a family area, the parlor was to be Paul's final resting place. Medicines, syringes, and additional medical supplies shrouded my antique buffet. A 2006 Christmas gift from Paul, "The Divine Mercy" image graced the right side while holy candles and several rosaries rested nearby. With the house quiet and the kids in school, the ambiance seemed different somehow.

Zach and Jake were fifth and sixth graders at St. Boniface Elementary School. Chelsea, an eighth grader, attended Pope John High School in our home town of Elgin, where her dad graduated in 1972.

The atmosphere that morning filled the parlor with peace and tranquility. Physical and mental exhaustion overwhelmed me. With eyes closed, I laid awake absorbing the stillness of the moment, pondering how much cancer transformed our lives.

Paul longed to spend his remaining time with his family and in his familiar surroundings. It was crucial that the children be with their father daily, except for unexpected hospitalization for surgeries and complications.

God lavished blessings on us with an additional 184 days, six hours and thirty minutes with Paul. The hassles and stress of driving to a nearby hospital or nursing home every day after school and weekends deemed nonexistent. Paul resided at the farm for the kids and me, all four thousand, four hundred twenty-two hours and thirty minutes.

Earlier happier times, Paul joked how someday, in our old age, he would be my caregiver. I exhibited numerous aches and pains and was the one falling apart. His kidding often suggested the remarkable traits and positive attributes of "his second wife." Paul's new and improved version of this fantasy woman didn't materialize. Sometimes our joking concluded in a light conversation whether we should again marry if the other would die; divorce never entered our discussion. Time ran out. The questions weren't answered!

Prior to cancer, Paul and I had an enjoyable teasing argument back and forth between us, unaware of the presence of five-year-old Jake who took our conversation to heart. Feelings threatened, immersed in tears and while hugging our legs together, *"Don't get a divorce. Don't get a divorce!"*

It seems essential for children to witness the connection and devotion between their parents, and with this bond they too will experience love.

Paul's family history showed no signs of cancer. He loved his fruits, vegetables, and maybe an occasional cookie. I on the other hand was his opposite, I worshiped my sweets.

"Now Paul, when you get to Heaven, you make sure you come back and visit me or something, let me know you're around me." I remarked, serious but half joking as I straightened out his sheets and blankets.

"Never on earth will this ever happen!" I thought to myself.

Paul grinned, "I will, but I'll have to learn the rules first!"

He mentioned who he would encounter in Heaven: his friends and relatives who went before him. He wasn't sad about this. Paul's faith and trust in God displayed itself in the excitement and joy shown in his eyes. The smile on his face shined from the mere thought of seeing his cousins Stephanie and Joni, his dad Eddie, and hearing the boisterous laughter of friend, Fr. Ken Potts. He mentally displayed a long list of people he prearranged to see soon.

With each new challenge, there appeared to be less hope. Every hour generated emergency rooms, hospital stays, blood tests, surgery for a port, diverse doctors, and exclusive procedures. The days continuously ended up with heartbroken kids.

The latest medicines possessed unexpected side effects. The pain increased beyond Paul's physical strength. One medication triggered diarrhea, while another inconsistently instigated painful constipation which only could be eased with the help of a committed hospice nurse at three in the morning.

Time worked against us as Paul deteriorated hourly. He attempted to eat, but nothing tasted good. Unwanted outcomes from medicines and the cancer worsening resulted in the food and drink not staying down.

It seemed like every half hour or less, day and night, Paul threw up large amounts of blood. I held the pail for him after it became impossible for him to do it alone. Immediately after his ungodly torture ceased for a short time, I wiped the food and blood from his chapped lips, t-shirt and fingers. Self-absorbed and vanity entered the picture. I prayed God had someone for me when I got to this point in my life!

I sensed a mental breakdown at hand. My mind and body stretched beyond human endurance but unknowingly, his grace kept me going. Each exhausting second was an explosion materializing within and around me. A giant volcano demanded to erupt continuously, to spit all of my vile anger, frustration, and weariness over everyone and everything surrounding me. The pending blast would unveil more harm than good. I was worn-out and exhausted. I held it in, except for a few hidden tears I wouldn't dare let Paul witness.

Paul continued to perform his best role-playings with our many visitors. He slyly misled his friends and family in believing he wasn't sick. In the awaited privacy of our home after everyone left, his smile left. Paul's body shrank and withered down into the bed and under the covers resulting from the pain he hid from everyone. He never complained.

A good friend of ours knew the uplifting marvels chocolate had on the heart and soul. She surprised us with a visit late one afternoon. Our conversation took its normal course of a light friendly discussion, joking around, and teasing as we feasted on this gratifying, earthly pleasure. Unanticipated, my emotions went erratic; from laughing, then crying, and erupting into a wounding explosion.

I resentfully exclaimed very cold insensitive words, "Paul, I can't take it anymore, *either die or get better.* I can't take the stress anymore. I just can't do it anymore!"

I hung my head from disgrace and shame and glanced toward Paul. He sat in his bed, eyes red and saturated with tears. We had been laughing. How could I have been this callous in blurting out dagger sharp words to a dying person? Especially someone whom I loved?

Compassion. He showed me kindness and mercy. Without drama, anger, or signs of self-pity, he showered me with simple, absolute compassion.

"I am so sorry." I sat beside him while we both cried and hugged each other. He told me that he understood and added how much he loved me. Tenderness and devotion unfolded during this blessed moment by him expressing a selfless and spiritual love. Agape love.

> Put on then, as God's chosen ones, holy and beloved, heartfelt compassion, kindness, humility, gentleness, and patience, bearing with one another and forgiving one another, if one has a grievance against another; as the Lord has forgiven you, so must you also do.
>
> Colossians 3:12-13

Chapter 4

The stomach acid began destroying his teeth. They became pitted and discolored as a result of losing their enamel. Every day, Paul made an effort to tell me how much he loved me or thanked me for helping him, even if it appeared in a whisper. Then, he would always smile.

Two days stand out in my mind of times which ripped and shredded five hearts into tiny pieces. We received several visits from hospice each week in the beginning. On one occasion, they suggested Chels, Jake, and Zach needed to be told sometime soon of their dad's impending death. The kids were aware of Paul's cancer. The puzzle pieces hadn't fit together yet of what the total picture included. I assume they were fully aware of the prognosis but didn't think or dwell on the final outcome.

The three of them were informed as a family in the parlor with the help of our hospice social worker. When they arrived in the parlor, I shared the startling news with them: "Dad has two weeks to live." Under a large pile, Paul became drenched in warm wet tears, broken hearts and disheartened offspring. This was so unfair. *God, I hope you know what you are doing!*"

God blessed us with fifty-one more days than the doctor's estimated date. But, as Paul's time came closer, the hospice nurses suggested I inform Chelsea, Jake and Zach to say their final goodbyes to their dad and tell him it was okay to "go." It would ease Paul's transition from this life to the next knowing that he has our permission to leave.

In my children's eyes, they had to perform something horrific: enlightening Daddy it was okay if he died! They went totally ballistic!

"No! We're not going to do it. We're not going to tell Dad he can die!" they screamed at me.

Life seemed to bring about only unpleasant tasks to complete, sometimes like homework. I replied, "We need to let Daddy know we will be okay. When the time comes for him to go, *he should go.*" They didn't understand. I didn't understand.

We gave Daddy our blessing to "go." Separately, each one of the kids told their dad he should go when the time came. They expressed their compassionate words with their many tears but not with their hearts. They didn't believe one word in what they conveyed to their dad. It became a job they had to finish.

The sorrow cut deep, unfathomable! Our family's grief consumed the very bottoms of our souls, where God *had never existed.* Where *was* God?

Paul wanted to die in a familiar place and around his family. I respected his unspoken wish where no discussions appeared necessary. We promised our love for one another years earlier and performed a renewal of vows with Fr. Dan Andrews, our parish priest, at our house several weeks before Paul died.

With the refreshing of our promises, special guests witnessed these vows! Excitement overflowed the parlor while our three blessings watched their mom and dad marry again for *their* first time! Positive energy and love filled our insecure lives as the kids videotaped and absorbed every promise Paul and I made years earlier.

The first wedding vows took place at St. Boniface Church in Elgin on September 21, 1991. We saw our future in each other's eyes. Filled with tears, joy and "new bride" jitters, I stumbled through my part of the declarations. Paul often laughed while teasing me about speaking my words wrong.

With cancer and Paul's impending death, our second exchange of marriage vows appeared as if they were budding and blossoming. They came alive. We continued living what we promised God. Marriage is about helping your spouse get to Heaven!

This second exchange of wedding vows became saturated with tears. I fumbled again with the same exact words. This time it wasn't about hopes and dreams, but death and loss of my husband. Each bittersweet word seemed more profound and more meaningful than they did the first time.

"…and will you continue to thank God for the gift of your children and bring them up according to the laws of Christ and His Church?"

"We do."

"Since it is the intent to renew your vows to declare your consent once again before God and His Church…" Father Andrews had us repeat our vows as we placed the rings on one another's finger. Paul would give me a quick glance and turn away, determined not to look at me in the eye. I envision it too hard on him seeing me suffer.

Profound love and devotion began radiating from my husband as he gazed into my eyes, "I, Paul, take you, Karen, once again to be my wife. I promise to be true to you in good times and in bad, in sickness and in health. I will love you and honor you *all* the days of my life."

I repeated the powerful words to my husband. They struck my heart as these promises were tested the past few months, but failed to change our marriage. Tears flowed.

"You have once again declared your consent, and the Lord and His Goodness strengthen your consent, and fill you both with His blessing. What God has joined, man *must not* and *will not* divide."

"Karen, take this ring as a sign of my love and fidelity in the name of the Father and the Son and the Holy Spirit." Paul spoke somberly.

Father Andrews then administered the Anointing of the Sick to Paul. Praying in silence he performed the laying on of hands, an ancient sign of the movement of the Holy Spirit to heal and save. Father anointed Paul's head and hands with oil blessed by the archbishop.

"Through this holy anointing, may the Lord in his love and mercy help you with the grace of the Holy Spirit. May the Lord who frees you from sin save you and raise you up."

This sacrament united Paul to the passion of Christ, giving him strength, peace, and courage to endure his last sufferings on earth.

Is anyone among you sick? He should summon the presbyters of the church, and they should pray over him and anoint (him) with oil in the name of the Lord, and the prayer of faith will save the sick person, and the Lord will raise him up. If he has committed any sin, he will be forgiven.

James 5:14-15

Paul commented on not worrying about himself. He agonized about our kids and me. How were we going to cope with losing him? He understood and foresaw a great amount of pain and grief in our future.

He mentioned phrases such as "I'm glad it's me dying and not you," "I would go crazy losing you," and "I wouldn't know how to care for the kids like you do." These statements were not selfish. Instead, they contained apprehension and concern, as a result of his love for us.

Paul's physical appearance changed with time. The blackish-brown hair and scarlet beard faded into a dull gray. His shoulders, arms, and face became thin, pale, and sunken in. His feet and legs, full of blood clots, felt numb except for a burning sensation. The blood thinners caused his brain tumor to hemorrhage. Paul faced heart failure, a stroke, or bleeding to death; a losing situation.

His once masculine, suntanned farm hands, which had lingered of dirt and grime under the fingernails turned frail and frosty. In order to keep all of his fingers, Paul only donned his wedding ring on Sundays and days he didn't do manual labor. However, during the months with cancer, the ring remained on his finger. With reverence, it was slid off before the casket was sealed. I glided it on my own finger and put my engagement and wedding diamonds away.

As Paul lay in his hospital bed, he loved the opportunities of watching evening sunsets from the large parlor windows facing the west. He witnessed the change in seasons as the array of greens silently turned to browns and golds, and gradually to a soft blanket of whiteness.

Chelsea, Jake, Zach, and I also witnessed *his* transformation in seasons as his tired body shriveled, withered, and died.

Unexpectedly and scaring the kids, Santa knocked hard on the kitchen door. Zach disappeared in the pantry while Chelsea and Jake scampered around the house energized. Mr. Claus entered the house looking for "one boy," and found Paul sitting up in bed in the back parlor.

While visiting, Santa teased Paul about receiving coal for Christmas one year. Then added, "Paul, I'm making plans on coming back next Christmas to see you again." Paul smiled and Santa continued, "Tom Osborn wants you to coach the Nebraska team. I heard you are a pretty good one!"

"My health isn't the best," Paul replied, grinning. He knew Santa well along with Mrs. Claus who smiled from the foot of the bed.

Not knowing if Paul would be with us for Christmas, Santa made an early "final" visit to our farm on a November evening. Assuming Santa came for our kids,

Paul became overwhelmed in tears when his surprise guest headed straight into the parlor bearing gifts of more miniature John Deere toys and to visit him!

Paul once commented, "I'll never be able to afford the big toys, at least I can enjoy the little ones."

After Mr. and Mrs. Claus left, Paul opened up his gifts as he began to weep. The kids piled on top of their dad and cried with him.

Later with tears still in his eyes he told me, "This is the best Christmas I ever had!"

Thanks, Santa and Mrs. Claus!!!

I received a phone call one day in December from Pope John High School. Chelsea, her eighth grade classmates, several teachers and their husbands wanted to come out to the house.

After arriving at the farm, they jumped out of cars and pickups, full of energy, enthusiasm and Christmas spirit. Amongst them, they brought a variety of cookies and hot apple cider.

With rapid speed, they decorated our front yard, the large wrap-around porch, and each tree and bush in sight with hundreds of colorful lights and Christmas decorations. The blessings from this day graced our family with warm memories of Paul's last Christmas season.

Toward the end of their visit, we were embellished with several Christmas carols. Smiles and tranquilly radiated from Paul's hospital bed. He watched and listened while Chelsea's class, full of grins and giggles (including the boys!), fully garbed in heavy coats, mittens, and hats sang in unison, or at least trying too!

From the opposite side of the decorated parlor windows, Paul immersed himself into their positive energy and enthusiasm for life. He knew his next Christmas would be celebrated with Jesus in Heaven.

Days later, he quietly asked me to pull the blinds down on all of the windows, thus making his room dark. The only visible port to his outside world was shut. His request surprised me. He loved the outdoors: its sensation of crispness in the early morning air to the silence of a setting sun. This moment would be his final time to see outside. The brain tumor persistently pressed on his right eye, causing it to bulge from its socket. The daylight resulted in pain in his eyes and head. The bulging also created double vision.

This seemed a major turning point for Paul. With him unable and no longer desiring to view nature, I could feel him slowly pulling himself inward into his own spiritual domain. Concerns, anxieties, and interests of this material world were irrelevant. As he changed, I realized that all material belongings, all worldly matter, and all social status didn't matter. All of it became insignificant; all of it except Paul's relationship with *Him.*

Christmas morning 2007 was humbling. Our first glimpse wasn't of the tree or the presents. Entering the living room and parlor area, Paul was sitting up in bed attentive, waiting on Chels, Jake, Zach, and me to wake up. In earlier years, it had been our kids waking Paul and me up early to open presents. With shimmering eyes, he was ready to celebrate Christmas with his family.

"I am really surprised I am still here. I thought I would be dead this morning." This comment didn't surprise me. With the many visits from hospice, I occasionally heard *with love,* "I'm surprised Paul is still with us" and "what he is going through, he shouldn't be here." I truly sense he fought to be with us his last Christmas on earth and witness the beginning of a new year.

God blessed us with the best Christmas present ever. Paul pulled himself inward again as the day progressed, and as his pain progressed and he tired.

Paul lived simple. His collection of John Deere tractors, guns and gun cabinet, and the many sports games he attended or watched did not matter. The few acres of land he owned, money in the bank, and small herd of cattle all proved unimportant now. He wasn't going to take anything with him when he died.

> As it is written: "Whoever had much did not have more, and whoever had little did not have less."
>
> 2 Corinthians 8:15

Paul's thoughts gradually became restricted "into himself." He no longer believed it was crucial to confide in me about worldly concerns or matters dealing with our kids. He contemplated on other essential factors, most likely issues God would gaze upon with fondness. As each day progressed, Paul grasped God's eternal hand with more confidence and trust, hopefully blessed with spiritual protection and divine shelter.

Paul lost the capability of getting out of bed. His lone kidney failed and toxic fluids filled his lower body. The morphine increased every few days along with his pain. He became an inspiration because not once did we hear him complain or ask, *"Why me?"*

We strived to give him many of his lasts, including a slow dance, a tractor drive, an early birthday, and basketball and volleyball games. They were memories that soothingly mended our own broken hearts. Hugs, kisses, and "I love yous" filled our time with Paul. Our greatest hope and desire was to have just one more day with him, never knowing if the next morning we would find him lifeless.

Even though we were blessed with additional time to spend with Paul, the evenings seemed worse than daytime hours. Every night, at least one of the kids ended up in a pool of tears, mingled with their grief, stress, heartache, and homework. As I held them tightly, while striving to manage my own sorrow, I made futile attempts to console their fragmented souls. My heart shattered into a million pieces when watching my children ache from the agony they carried.

I often asked myself, "How did Mary handle the pain as her heart collapsed while witnessing her son's suffering and death?" I couldn't imagine her grief.

After praying the Divine Mercy Chaplet, I continued to reflect on what life bestowed on us. I lay wrapped in a blanket on the couch next to Paul's hospital bed during the last days. Meanwhile, he often stared into space with a blank look. It left me questioning whether he was sleeping or visiting the other side of eternity.

With my eyes closed, Heaven gently graced me as I rested.

A cool touch of a delicate breeze swept my forehead and nose, like an angel's wing brushing my face.

Breathtaking!

And no, it wasn't the ceiling fan or furnace!

> Are they not all ministering spirits sent to serve, for the sake of those who are to inherit salvation?
>
> Hebrews 1:14

Chapter 5

"*There is so much stuff in my mind. There is so much to think about. Things keep flashing in my mind. It makes me feel like I'm going crazy!*" Paul remarked to me early one morning.

Earlier in the week, unusual noises came from the parlor.

"What's that noise? What are you doing, Paul?" I asked in a panic.

"There are people in the house, and they're scaring me!" he replied as he attempted to get out of bed and out of the room. I decided to put up the bed side rails. Paul's legs couldn't support him any longer. With an absence of control and sensation from the waist down, his abdomen, hips, butt, and legs were tight and swollen with fluids. Flight, a natural result of panic and fright, might cause Paul to pull himself down out of the bed. It would be impossible for me to get him back in by myself.

It was difficult for Paul to breath during and after any small activity. At first, he used the toilet stool normally. But as time progressed, I lifted the toilet seat so he could sit on the cold porcelain area. His "bottom" eventually overlapped this, consequently from the fluid in his lower body. Going to the restroom was an exhausting chore and something we had taken for granted!

As Paul's health declined, he no longer walked to the bathroom. He was given a hand held plastic container to use when lying in bed. Paul started having trouble staying awake. Several times I found him asleep while holding his urinal upright, trying not to spill its contents. He tried to be a perfect patient. He then graduated to a catheter which emptied into a bag at the base of his bed. Because his kidneys were shutting down, his urine emerged dark and brown.

It is amazing how I have flashbacks on comments he said or things he did as I write this book. Incidents I didn't write in my journals, and I have long forgotten.

One day Paul told me, "I don't want to be a bother or to make more work for you." I was exhausted, but I would do it all over again for him. I gave Paul, Chels, Jake, and Zach everything I had, every last drop, all of the energy I possessed within me and continued to squeeze out even more.

My eyes were opened to the extreme love a caregiver pours out on their beloved. Others observe these deeds of mercy, but it takes the actual experience to completely feel its magnitude.

This also applies with the death of a loved one. When you personally have gone through a loss and have been mounted at the bottom of that cross, only then will you sense its immensity.

"Dear God, I could not have done it without you!"

Paul made a new friend: a big, brown dog. It contrasted with rat terriers, the only dogs to ever live on the family farm.

Paul looked under his sheet and announced, "There he goes. He's okay!" and "He's behind the bed!"

Paul continued telling me his convincing stories with enthusiasm. Once, the dog and he jumped into the pickup and drove to a field where his cousins, Bill and Red, were spring planting. Another time, Paul wanted to get the crops in fast because cousins Red, Bill and Dave were almost finished harvesting their quarters. This dog seemed to be with Paul nonstop. Adventures took place in the fields, riding in the combine, or journeying in the tractor. Paul's new companion, and best friend, gave him the blessings of comfort and reassurance his last few days.

After a while, I decided to go along with Paul's farfetched story. He once again commented about the dog behind his bed. I told him I spotted his faithful companion. Paul smiled and softly said, "*Stop it!*" He knew I couldn't see his dog. I only tried to pacify him.

Paul's hospital bed sat in the center of the parlor. It established an easy access for administering meds, repositioning him so he wouldn't develop bed sores, and give him bed baths and food massages. Chels, Jake, and Zach could easily crawl in with their dad at any time. On occasion they would take a nap, read him a story, or even watch Pope John High School play a winning championship game in Lincoln.

Life became more tolerant for Paul after a surgery placed a "port" on his upper chest. The hospice nurses showed me how to dispense medicines through this blessing and keep everything sterile. Paul no longer had to get shots intravenously.

"Karen, I think I'm going crazy. I just want to go home."

I occasionally gave him medicine which reduced the agitation. He felt death even more imminent. At some point the last months, I don't recall when or how, but I realized it was time for Paul to "go."

He was tired. I was tired.

Lord, please take him Home!

> Can any of you by worrying add a single moment to your life-span?
>
> Matthew 6:27

Chapter 6

Today is January 7th, 2008. A normal evening comprised of feeding Paul and preparing him for bed. I would give him a back and foot rub, and finish the night by dispensing his meds. Lucy, a hospice staff member, spoiled Paul with the foot rubs!

Every evening, we prayed the Divine Mercy Chaplet. Tonight held no exception. We gathered around Paul, each grasping a rosary and taking turns leading the prayer. Holy candles set the mood as the only source of light. It doesn't take long to say, but is beautiful and powerful.

Paul, in the final fourth stage of cancer, didn't pray with us. Maybe he listened. Paul lay silently, in a different world. He stared into space.

Earlier in the day he asked me, "Is there anybody else in the house?"

"No, we are the only ones here."

"Are you sure?" I kept reassuring him we were alone.

After praying that evening, I told the kids to finish their homework. Instantly, Paul became terrified. He seemed to be observing shapes which the kids and I assumed were angels. He screamed at us, "Everybody stay and say the Chaplet again! Keep praying!"

Paul prayed fervently, saying every word as fast as he could, *"For the sake of His sorrowful passion, have mercy on us and on the whole world."*

His eyes flashed as they scanned the parlor and living room in all directions. They were on fire. His heart pounded.

After finishing the second Chaplet, I once again told the kids to finish their homework. I had little concern because I believed we were in the presence of angels. Chelsea edged around the corner of Paul's bed to place her rosary on the buffet. With wide eyes, Paul angrily screamed at her, "Chels, get away from there. There's one there!"

He continued in panic, "They are black and brown. They're not angels; they're ugly!"

"They're peeking around the parlor doors," Paul exclaimed. We were confused; we didn't understand. The kids were terrified.

Paul started whispering, "…so they won't hear us! Call Father Andrews!" I was very confused and did not realize the need of calling Father so late at night.

Frustrated with me, Paul shouted, "Call Father Andrews now!"

I sat on a bar stool next to his bed. I watched his eyes follow an invisible creature floating beside me up over my head. I thought, *"This is not the morphine!"*

Fr. Dan Andrews arrived at the farm within minutes. He rushed in and stated, "There's a battle going on!"

Father blessed Paul and our family. He recited prayers casting out demons as he sprinkled holy water throughout our home. When Father Andrews first entered our house, the spirits commenced to leave. Peace instantly surrounded Paul. He saw no more while Father stayed at the house, and Father advised us to always have holy water. Fr. Andrews explained that he heard of these happenings, but never witnessed until now. It also happened to be our first time, and hopefully our last!

Father Andrews helped us during this spiritual crisis. He often came out to the farm to celebrate Holy Mass with close family and friends, and give Paul the Sacraments of Anointing of the Sick or Confession.

He informed me, "Paul is suffering for other people".

Later that night, when the kids were sleeping in our bedroom, I asked Paul if he saw anything more.

He whispered, "A man and a woman are in the living room. I don't know who they are, but they seem nice. They are laughing at you." He quietly giggled and covered his mouth like a little boy with a secret.

He observed this veiled couple who shared our living room and parlor with us. It exposed the reality of the close knit connection we all have concerning time and eternity.

With calmness, I continued preparing Paul for bed. I told him, "They can laugh all they want. They can't harm us. This is a house where God is."

Especially at the end of life, Satan strives for your soul. Fr. Andrews later told me Paul decided long ago whose side he was on: God's!

When Paul awoke the next afternoon, his worn First Communion rosary was still draped in his hands from the horrid night before.

"Lord, I can't do another one of those nights!"
Jesus told Sister Faustina:

> Oh, how much I am hurt by a soul's distrust!
> Such a soul professes that I am Holy and Just,
> but does not believe that I am Mercy and does
> not trust in My Goodness. Even the devils
> glorify My Justice but do not believe in My
> Goodness. (300)
>
> After the adoration, half way to my cell, I
> was surrounded by a pack of huge black dogs
> who were jumping and howling and trying
> to tear me to pieces. I realized that they were
> not dogs but demons. One of them spoke up
> in a rage, "Because you have snatched so many
> souls away from us this night, we will tear you
> to pieces." I answered, "if that is the will of the
> most merciful God, tear me to pieces, for I
> have justly deserved it, because I am the most
> miserable of sinners, and God is ever holy, just,
> and infinitely merciful." To these words all the
> demons answered as one, "Let us flee, for she
> is not alone; the Almighty is with her!" And
> they vanished like dust...while I continued on
> my way to my cell undisturbed. (320) I united
> my sufferings with the sufferings of Jesus and
> offered them for myself and for the conversion
> of souls who do not trust in the goodness of
> God. Suddenly, my cell was filled with black
> figures full of anger and hatred for me. One
> of them said, "Be damned, you and He who is
> within you, for you are beginning to torment
> us even in hell." As soon as I said, "And the

Word was made flesh and dwelt among us," the figures vanished in a sudden whir. (323)

And the LORD said to Satan, "Whence do you come?" Then Satan answered the LORD and said, "From roaming the earth and patrolling it."

Job 1:7

For our struggle is not with flesh and blood but with the principalities, with the powers, with the world rulers of this present darkness, with the evil spirits in the heavens.

Ephesians 6:12

Faith is the realization of what is hoped for and the evidence of things not seen.

Hebrews 11:1

Chapter 7

Tintern Retreat Center is a nourishing place to encounter people with the same Christian beliefs. Fr. William Safranek visited Tintern often, where he became good friends with Paul, the manager of Tintern. Tintern's ambiance would refresh and rejuvenate him. It is encircled by hilly woodlands and streams with a flawless environment for wild turkey, deer, and bald eagles. What a beautiful, never-ending panoramic countryside!

Fr. Safranek came out to our farm for a final visit. They both immersed themselves into a private conversation, confession, and all else needing to be said or done. The parlor portrayed a haven for them to expose their thoughts and prayers with one another and their lone God.

I spoke to Fr. Safranek earlier concerning the events that unfolded the night before. He seemed amazed and intrigued by this account. When his visits came to a close, he tried numerous times to depart, but he was always drawn back to Paul's side. He knew the final hour was approaching.

Paul struggled to inhale. An unforgettable sound, the "rattle," emerged deeply from his lungs and throat. Oxygen no longer portraying itself as an asset in breathing; it only prolonged his life and shoved death thoughtlessly to the side. Paul coughed up bubbly, bloody gunk from his fluid filled lungs. His upper body sunk in while his face looked distorted. He continuously "picked and pulled" at his clothing and bed sheets, a true indication his existence appeared to be ending.

I thought to myself, *"Why don't you just get up and stop putting on this act!"*

> In my Father's house there are many dwelling places. If there were not, would I have told you that I am going to prepare a place for you? And if I go and prepare a place for you, I will come back again and take you to myself, so that where I am you also may be.
>
> John 14:2-3

Chapter 8

Mark Schindler portrayed a hardworking farmer, devout Catholic, husband, and family man. Countless family and friend's alleged his vibrant life ended too quickly. An undetected heart defect inflicted and yet, blessed the Schindlers. In the prime of life, Mark and Peg supported and unconditionally loved their three maturing children. However, the old adage goes: "How do you make God laugh? Tell Him your future plans!"

Each individual, including you, lives a personal story to share. Peg and her family had an exceptional account of their grueling journey. They now perceive life in a new fashion. Individually, they are managing their gift in diverse manners. God blessed them with new insights at the twinkling of Mark's departure. Peg, Melissa, Jake, and Ross are challenged each and every single day to trust and to rely on him more, even though they don't understand his ways. They take less for granted and love harder. God desired their unadulterated attention!

God smiles when he uses suffering and adversity to open our unseeing eyes and our impenetrable hearts. It's a loving and patient smile. He knows exactly where he is taking you. What we contemplate as misery and hardship is *always* a grace filled blessing in disguise. As humans, we are incapable of comprehending it in the first moment. Each trial is another step closer to him, *if we let it.*

Peg and her oldest son, Jake, left our house one Sunday morning after administering Holy Communion to Paul and me. I felt a deep-seated intuition that Peg's visit was still in progress. Something wasn't finished as they drove out of our driveway onto the country road.

> His disciples asked him, "Rabbi, who sinned, this man or his parents, that he was born blind?" Jesus answered, "Neither he nor his parents sinned; it is so that the works of God might be made visible through him."
>
> John 9:2-3

Chapter 9

AseraCare Hospice from O'Neill, Nebraska was a godsend. As an immense undertaking, their main objective of keeping Paul comfortable his final months appeared challenging. The concept of strangers in our home seemed unappealing, but with time and trust, friendships developed.

With these new companionships, our conversations informed me Peg Schindler needed to visit Paul once more. Spiritually and emotionally, she deemed it necessary to complete her prior visit.

During the last months, we received hundreds of phone calls. The front door consumed a constant flow of friends and family, sometimes bumping into one another as they passed through our threshold.

With the overwhelming pressures of life and with little time to ourselves, temptations lured me. I wanted to unplug the phones, pull the window shades, lock all the doors, and pretend we weren't home. I thank God I didn't because each individual brought our family immeasurable blessings.

Our home budded and blossomed with friends, family, laughter and tears. Our house busted at its seams with sincere compassion and charity. We witnessed and experienced a surplus of unconditional love and kindness only a small town and surrounding communities in Nebraska could reveal.

When faced with uncomfortable situations, one can never tell how we will react to it, and we should never judge another's actions.

On one occasion, Paul's steadfast friend hung up on him. She couldn't endure speaking with him; life seemed too painful for her to face. Another buddy asked, "How could you do this to *me?*" He took it personally.

Several close friends couldn't force themselves one last visit. The words, pain, death, and friendship were not considered an option in life or even in the same sentence. Final visits with Paul were too unbearable and uncomfortable to experience, so they didn't take place.

Peg acted differently; an unfinished mission consumed her thoughts. I called her at work, asking if she needed to visit with Paul. With her high intentions on completing this aspiration, she arrived at the farm almost immediately.

I accompanied Peg into our parlor where she saw him days before.

"Paul, Peg is here to see you."

Paul hadn't spoken a word all day. With his mouth and lips dry, tongue swollen, and jaw stiff, the slightest amount of speaking produced a high hurdle for him to clear.

His searching eyes found her near his bed.

"Hi Peg," came out of Paul's parched mouth so lucidly. He held her complete attention. With a solemn personal request, Peg bid Paul to relay private and personal matters she didn't get a chance to express to

Mark. She felt guilty taking my time away from Paul. I explained that we had our "I love yous" and "Goodbyes" a thousand times.

She needed to complete this task before Paul was unable to comprehend or answer her. Peg asked me to stay, but I didn't. I closed the two heavy oak French doors behind me. The parlor once again became a haven, but this time with Paul, Peg, and Mark. After several minutes, she entered the kitchen in tears. She sensed Mark's and God's presence.

I sent her back, with a gift of more time with Paul. Peg felt complete tranquility when she finished. She departed from our house overjoyed and at peace. The words expressed and the passions experienced left with Paul, and it genuinely originated from the heart, Peg's heart.

> Have no anxiety at all, but in everything, by prayer and petition, with thanksgiving, make your requests known to God. Then the peace of God that surpasses all understanding will guard your hearts and minds with Christ Jesus.
>
> Philippians 4:6-7

Chapter 10

Tear of Compassion

Several months after Paul's death, Peg Schindler ambled up to the top of the gym bleachers where I was sitting. The junior high basketball crowd had not yet congregated, so we had a chance to visit alone. Peg chose to unveil new and enlightening details to me.

Peg spoke of the message Paul was to relay to Mark. Paul's head lay stiffly on his pillow while he listened to Peg. She noticed a tear roll slowly down the side of his tired face as she confided in him.

He grasped the meaning and recognized the importance of Peg's message. He perceived and sensed her pain in missing Mark and the immeasurable passion she felt for her husband. I truly believe Mark received and cherishes his wife's words of love.

The Box of Love

One afternoon, as Paul lay in bed he said, "Karen, I have a box here on my lap. It holds everything your dad never told you."

I questioned Paul of its contents. Smiling, Paul replied, "Your dad loves you."

Paul detected and touched this hypothetical box. He recognized the value and importance within it. After surprising me with this unexpected testimonial, I lay my head down on Paul's chest and wept while he stroked my hair, consoling me. How did he know this simple statement of love would affect me so much?

My dad and mom raised eleven children on the minimal profits of one quarter of land. This is an exceptional feat compared to today's standard of living. My one younger sister, Annette, died nineteen days old from pneumonia.

Dad wasn't brought up to say "I love you." His parents never verbalized it to him or his siblings. He didn't express these words to his own children and continued handing down the old German custom. For him, it wasn't an easy undertaking.

"The best thing I ever did was to have you kids," we sometimes heard dad remark to us as he grinned.

My siblings and I are fully aware of our dad's love for us. When quite young, I often caught glimpses of my Dad praying on his knees in the dark back room before going to bed. He is still a man of prayer and faith. He's a part of the older generation of Christians who pray behind closed doors, giving God homage at the close of the day.

> But when you pray, go to your inner room, close the door, and pray to your Father in secret. And your Father who sees in secret will repay you.
>
> Matthew 6:6

Chapter 11

P aul was fighting for air. Sleep apnea showed its horrid face. The breathing stopped for what feels like an eternity, and then finally a large gasp of air was sucked in. Each labored breath seemed to be Paul's last.

I realized this "breath" is the "breath of God," the same given to Adam and Eve. Paul's heart ran rampant and soon slowed down, barely beating. This happened over and over again. Paul couldn't hold his head up the last few days, his chin fell down to his shoulder. I tried to use towels and blankets for supports, but they didn't offer any relief.

Before going to bed, Chelsea trembled as she walked into the parlor to say goodnight to her dad as she did every night. She knew his time was almost complete.

"Dad, will you be there for me when I go to Heaven?" she asked with a pounding heart.

Paul breathed, "Yes, Chels!" This would be Chelsea's last conversation with her dad.

I leaned closer to Paul's weary face. He needed to tell me something crucial. In a mumble, Paul whispered, *"I love you!"* as he squeezed my hand.

"I love you too, Hun!" I said, grasping his hand in return.

He commenced to embrace Chelsea, Jake, and Zach's hands. Days earlier when it was getting difficult for Paul to speak; I suggested he squeeze our hands as a sign of his love. Life is soon to expire!

Being infuriated with God questioned my faith. Where is he? Where is this great "ocean of mercy" I heard about?

My prayers for Paul's peaceful death intensified day after day. Where was it? How could *he* abandon us when we needed him? A merciful God wouldn't put us through this hell!

"There's not much time left." Paul whispered in my ear. He barely got his words out. It took all the energy he could muster.

Our Lord said to Saint Faustina:

> …encourage souls to say the Chaplet which I have given you…(1541).Whoever will recite it will receive great mercy at the hour of death. (687)…when they say this chaplet in the presence of the dying, I will stand between my Father and the dying person, not as the Just Judge but as the Merciful Savior (1541). Priests will recommend it to sinners as their last hope of salvation. Even if there were a sinner most hardened, if he were to recite this chaplet only once, he would receive grace from my infinite mercy. I desire to grant unimaginable graces to those souls who trust in My mercy (687)…Through the Chaplet you will obtain everything, if what you ask for is compatible with My will (1731).

Prayer exhausted me, I couldn't do it anymore. I prayed one final time for a peaceful death. God knew my breaking point. Paul instantaneously consumed peace. *"Thank you Father, for hearing my prayer."*

Our Lord also said:

> I promise that the soul that will venerate this image will not perish. I also promise victory over its enemies already here on earth, especially at the hour of death. I myself will defend it as My own glory. (Diary 48)

> The Lord God formed the man out of the clay of the ground and blew into his nostrils the breath of life, and so the man became a living being.
>
> Genesis 2:7

Chapter 12

The air was cold as the sun came up on Friday, January 11, 2008. I checked on Paul several times through the night and early morning hours. I knew the time was close. His heart beat and breathing were almost undetectable. It was time for all the prayers from family and friends to continue their blessings. I didn't have the strength to pray anymore.

Earlier in the morning, I pulled Paul's bed up against the couch where I slept so I could hear him if he moved or made any sound. My plans were to lie near him and not fall asleep. I wanted to keep vigil.

I failed miserably. The apostles in the garden and I have one thing in common: we couldn't stay awake, not for Jesus, and not for Paul. I felt overwhelmed with disappointment, with my pathetic human weakness.

A little before 6:30 a.m., I awoke. Paul was gone. His body warmth was fading away slowly.

Cancer didn't kill him. He died from a failed heart, and I, from a broken heart!

Paul loved early mornings. The time he always rose to start a new day paralleled with the time he rose to greet his *Father*.

Gently, I woke Chelsea, Jake, and Zach a little after. My bedroom transformed into their dorm room, following the shock of our unwanted evening visitors.

I calmly told them their dad passed away. My young children gazed at me with wide questioning eyes, then slowly they crawled out of bed, not knowing what to anticipate. Chelsea later expressed, "When I heard you open the door, I woke up, and I felt and knew that Dad was no longer with us."

They treaded softly on the oak floors into the parlor. No one spoke. They stood alongside his bed, gazing at their dad with hesitance. They timidly followed my prompting of holding their dad's still-lukewarm hand.

New life conquered death. Mortal words cannot justify the ambiance experienced that morning.

Paul lay motionless.

The room's energy overflowed with tranquil peace and stillness. Time felt frozen alongside of eternity.

> He will wipe away every tear from their eyes, and there shall be no more death or mourning, wailing or pain, [for] the old order has passed away.
>
> Revelation 21:4

> Behold, I tell you a mystery. We shall not all fall asleep, but we shall all be changed, in an instant, in the blink of an eye, at the last trumpet.
>
> 1 Corinthians 15:51-52

> When his spirit departs he returns to his earth; on that day his plans perish.
>
> Psalm 146:4

Insert from CaringBridge website, CarePages.com
Tuesday, December 11, 2007 11:09 AM, CST

Paul, I just wanted to share some thoughts
with you. We live in a world that does just
about anything to get out of or avoid suffering.
We, most of the time, have little idea of how
to handle it. We don't like to talk about it and
especially to those who are going through it. But
I am going to talk to you about it. I remember
watching Pope John Paul II live through his
last years and how he made everyone who
encountered him look at suffering and how
it can be lived. You are a strong faith person
and one of the things we all believe or should
believe is that suffering is redemptive. I think
John Paul showed that there are few prayers
you can say that even comes close to a day of
suffering that is offered up to The Lord. There
is a statement that St. Paul (your patron saint)
makes that tells those who suffer that they are
part of the real redemptive sacrifice that Jesus
offered up on Calvary. That Paul is your special
gift. I don't think a lot of people are given that
gift and if they are they refuse to see it in that
light. I believe that to see ones suffering as a
prayer is one of the most powerful signs of how
much God loves you. There are few of us who
have suffered at the level you are at, but I want
you to know that our prayers are that you take
this gift and use it to its fullest. You have been
a special sign for a lot of us who have watched
you travel this journey. Maybe it isn't the end.

God could change it, but if it doesn't change and this is the end of your life know that as a man of faith you have given a beautiful sign to the rest of us and when our time comes I pray I will be given the same gift and will live it out as well as you have. You are in my prayers every day. During Advent, we are all about preparing for the coming of the Lord. We share that preparation with you in a real way this Advent. I ask God's blessing on you and your family during this Advent time and your time of preparation.

We Love you Much,
George and Mary Shoemaker
(Uncle and Aunt of Paul)
Denver, CO

Chapter 13

At approximately 6:30 a.m. on January 11th 2008, Paul experienced God. He was prepared. I believed the previous six months seemed challenging for our family. A bright Sunday morning so long ago began our absolute mourning. An unfamiliar road in our extensive journey unfolded. Paul wrestled personal sufferings and confirmation of his own death. We agonized in watching him slowly suffer and die while trying to possess some amount of "normal" in our lives. I assumed life to be easier after he *would* depart and the hardest part would be finished. I could not have been farther from the truth.

I don't remember who I called, but two of our hospice nurses, Kim Wells and Michele Stearns arrived at the house to prepare Paul's body for the funeral home. They closed the parlor doors behind them. Once again, the parlor became a haven to ready the body, not the soul, for its next phase. Being naïve to this experience and what it entailed left me tentative. I escaped to the bathroom to shower. I discovered later, Erin, our hospice social worker, was consoling the kids in our basement; I had no recollection of her being at the house.

Paul's soul rested in the presence of its creator. Judgment day ultimately arrived.

I recall turning the water on as hot as I could tolerate. I lingered in the shower for the longest time needing to be cleansed of something, but I couldn't comprehend what. I sobbed. I wept loud, from the very depths of my soul. I thought, "*It's over*," like Jesus revealed on his cross before he died. My purpose in life appeared over. With Paul's life departed and his suffering finished, I sensed desolation and overwhelming darkness.

The farm house seemed to cast down her eyes in sorrow and reverence, and the land and the large red barn nodded their final goodbyes to Paul. He lay peacefully on the gurney, covered with pure white sheets and a rosary in his hands. Paul was escorted out of the same door he had entered through as a new born son fifty-three years earlier cradled by his mom. With his soul absent, Paul seemed empty. It is comparable to a vacant cocoon after the butterfly departs. I felt numb and as if my whole being severed in half.

> He said in reply, "Have you not read that from the beginning the Creator 'made them male and female' and said, 'For this reason a man shall leave his father and mother and be joined to his wife, and the two shall become one flesh'? So they are no longer two, but one flesh. Therefore, what God has joined together, no human being must separate."
>
> Matthew 19:4-6

Chapter 14

The hard hitting news of reoccurring cancer hit without remorse. After several weeks, Paul sensed the distress taking its toll on me. Noticing my head and shoulders hanging low and my heart drooping even lower he asked me to see a doctor. Perhaps a prescription would help me deal with the pain and stress of life. His concern focused more on my welfare than his own.

Paul was unaware of the countless occasions I grieved; he didn't need to know. I often pulled into the nearby rural cemetery where Paul would eventually rest. After crying, I dried my tears and headed for home as if nothing happened. "Happy pills" eased the upper layer of pain; to mask the deep rooted sorrow. The medication helped me display a phony smile to simulate life seemingly manageable. It wasn't. I smiled on the outside, yet wounded and battered on the inside.

The first weeks of being at home from Omaha, Paul and I slept in our bedroom. After numerous days, he reclined in his chair and then recoiling to a hospital bed. The pain intensified as he labored to get his breath after little physical exertion or lying flat in bed. A comfortable sleeping position became difficult to locate. The tumors were spreading in his bones and in his lungs making discomfort his only alternative. As cancer ravaged his lungs, Paul's coughing escalated.

With each stab, Paul pressed a pillow firmly to his ribs to soften the sharp jolts surging through his body.

Once Paul moved to the hospital bed, we utilized our cell phones to access one another during the nights. With my phone on "buzz" Paul would frequently notify me when he needed an increase of morphine, or a quick trip to the bathroom before an unpleasant soiled accident befell all over the wooden floor. I often gave him back or leg massages to relieve pain and cramps or help him hold his puke bucket while he filled it with tinted red fluids. Other times he only needed someone to talk too.

One night after my phone buzzed, and being in such a frantic to get to Paul, I jumped out of bed and ran head first into a large oak dresser. At the moment of brutal impact I didn't laugh, but as time passes, all memories including the very raw ones seem to soften and sweeten.

Blessings from prayers and faith fortified us. The *Divine Mercy Chaplet* continued to play an important role in our family. Before Paul died, we recited this Chaplet faithfully every night, and I, during the day praying for some kind of miracle.

After Pauls' death, anger set in. I cared nothing of this "mercy" topic. My defiance refused God and everything mercy stood for. *God didn't care about healing Paul, why should I care about helping Him out!—as if He needs my help*!

Jesus said to St Faustina;

> At three o'clock, implore My mercy, especially for sinners; and, if only for a brief moment, immerse yourself in My Passion, particularly in My abandonment at the moment of agony.

This is the hour of great mercy for the whole world... In this hour, I will refuse nothing to the soul that makes a request of Me in virtue of My Passion (Diary, 1320).

...As often as you hear the clock strike the third hour, immerse yourself completely in My mercy, adoring and glorifying it; invoke its omnipotence for the whole world, and particularly for poor sinners; for at that moment mercy was opened wide for every soul. In this hour you can obtain everything for yourself and for others for the asking; it was the hour of grace for the whole world — mercy triumphed over justice. (1572)

I questioned Fr. Andrews about my hostile thoughts and my struggles preparing for the Three O'clock Prayer Hour for Divine Mercy Sunday. He believed Satan placed those undesirable beliefs in my head. I later conveyed to God it was all in his hands, I wasn't interested this year. I didn't have the energy or the determination, but God understood. God knows our tears. He understands the pain of losing a friend.

When Mary came to where Jesus was and saw him, she fell at his feet and said to him, "Lord, if you had been here, my brother would not have died." When Jesus saw her weeping and the Jews who had come with her weeping, he became perturbed and deeply troubled, and said, "Where have you laid him?"

They said to him, "Sir, come and see."

And Jesus wept.

John 11:32-35

Chapter 15

Numerous background incidents are to be acknowledged and shared with you before continuing this script. The kids and I didn't contemplate on any of these occurrences. Life continued to transpire around us. I believe everything happens for a reason and that coincidences are nonexistent.

Game or Not

I drove Chels, Jake, and Zach to the Girls' state basketball finals in Lincoln after Paul passed away. It was a challenge to disengage from life's tense routine. On our route to the tournament, our Chrysler's oil light started flashing and wouldn't quit. I prayed the car would keep running and suggest we return home. The alert ceased to blink immediately on the way back home. The car was later serviced and the repairers concluded no malfunctions existed.

Paul's Favorites

Paul's favorite scents were of a recent rain shower, fresh cut alfalfa and silage, and harvest. Every deep-rooted farmer is acquainted with these distinct smells of the land. The fragrance Paul loved above all is of new born babies: their natural scents as well as the aroma of baby powder. He especially enjoyed them on his own children. We often laughed about the "real" robust stench of babies!

Public Dread

After Paul died, I dreaded going out in public without him. Who to sit with and where were questions I didn't have answers for. I believed people constantly observed me and viewed me as "that poor widow." I assumed my friends were apprehensive sitting next to me. They wouldn't know what a conversation would entail. Just the thought or suggestion of attending a concert or a sports event placed me in a full-blown anxiety attack. I took for granted Paul would always be at my side or at least until we got older.

You complete me

One Christmas, I received a love letter from Paul. I cried while reading the personal and beautiful words. Besides expressing those three simple words, Paul wrote, "You make me complete." He smiled at me while I finished. His words infiltrated into the depth of my heart and my soul. This simple hand written note bestowed the greatest gift I ever received, expressions extending from the innermost part of Paul's heart.

> Rejoice always. Pray without ceasing. In all circumstances give thanks, for this is the will of God for you in Christ Jesus. Do not quench the Spirit. Do not despise prophetic utterances. Test everything; retain what is good. Refrain from every kind of evil.
>
> 1 Thessalonians 5:16-21

Chapter 16

"Paul wants you to know he's okay" and "he's with his big brown dog!" Sandy revealed.

I was not aware this distant cousin existed. Sandy lived along the East Coast. Certain individuals have the gift of speaking in tongue, healing the sick, or are slain in the spirit. Sandy had a gift of conversing with spirits since childhood. She assumed from a very early age everyone had this ordinary ability.

When we were little, my siblings and I learned to never mess with Ouija boards and séances. We were forbidden to see "The Exorcist." Our parents educated us to shy away entirely from everything involving spirits. I debated with myself whether I should hang the phone up or not. *"What am I getting into? This is weird!"*

Sandy continued, "Paul and my dad visited me last night. Paul said not to worry about the car. Nothing is wrong with it." She later added, "Paul loves the smell of new born babies. When you go to games and you are sitting on those bleachers, Paul is right beside you. He is there with you." No one knew these fears but me. My tears fell like torrential rains. She kept speaking, "He says you made him complete." This assertion could only come from Paul's love letter.

She then asked, "Did Paul give you a heart locket or something with a heart, two of something, maybe a bright light, a prayer or song?" Sandy knew nothing of the significances of her overwhelming words. She relayed the words she heard, and I was to interpret them. My tears poured at the mention of the brown dog, but at this description, I became awestruck.

It had to be The Divine Mercy Image, which included Jesus's heart and two bright rays and the Chaplet of Mercy in song. I was ecstatic! Paul had presented me with a framed picture the Christmas before. How could she know these details? I never spoke to her until this phone call. Sandy stated she had no inkling to what her visions or words meant. She was not familiar with the Divine Mercy.

I met Sandy's mom, Pat, several years earlier. Pat and my mom, Laura Mae, are first cousins. Paul appeared to Sandy the night before the phone call. She kept hearing, "Paul, Karen, tell Karen, tell Karen, Paul." Sandy didn't know a Paul and Karen, so she confided in her mom. My mom kept Pat informed on our family's situation. Pat immediately directed Sandy in our direction. That morning's phone call altered our family's outlook on life and on death. The dead are not dead; they are changed, they are transformed. An unseen dimension encircles us and many are unaware of a constant battle for our souls! We would be petrified in witnessing it. We are not alone.

> Jesus said to them in reply, "You are misled because you do not know the scriptures or the power of God. At the resurrection they neither marry nor are given in marriage but are like the angels in heaven. And concerning

the resurrection of the dead, have you not read what was said to you by God, 'I am the God of Abraham, the God of Isaac, and the God of Jacob'? He is not the God of the dead, but of the living."

Matthew 22:29-32

There are different kinds of spiritual gifts but the same Spirit; there are different forms of service but the same Lord; there are different workings but the same God who produces all of them in everyone. To each individual the manifestation of the Spirit is given for some benefit. To one is given through the Spirit the expression of wisdom; to another the expression of knowledge according to the same Spirit; to another faith by the same Spirit; to another gifts of healing by the one Spirit; to another mighty deeds; to another prophecy; to another discernment of spirits; to another varieties of tongues; to another interpretation of tongues. But one and the same Spirit produces all of these, distributing them individually to each person as he wishes.

1 Corinthians 12:4-11

Chapter 17

Following Paul's death, the kids and I commenced to noticing unexplainable incidents. These occurrences may seem trivial, but to us, they were inspiring and transcendent.

Crystals of Rain

It was a beautiful morning. The sun shone brightly as the kids played in the front yard and I hung clothes up to dry on the line near the back of the house. The heavens opened and sprinkled raindrops around us. This continued for several minutes. The kids wondered how this could be happening. No cloud hung in the sky. The rain showered down on us like miniature crystals, glistening from the sun.

Problems of the Heart

My mom dealt with serious health problems, including several blockages. She endured a triple bypass surgery. I was, again, mad at God. He got a hold of my attention the first time with Paul. Challenging my faith seemed to be his favorite pastime!

Since I needed to vent my anger, I walked down our country road crying and yelling at *Him*. On the walk back, I happened to look down toward the ground and discovered a heavy iron spike lying in the middle of our graveled road. How did I miss this six inch spear earlier? Awareness of this object graced in my hand helped me grasp the importance of our afflictions and sufferings. There are numerous crosses in one's lifetime, but they will never be as sincere or profound as *His!*

Tugging My Heart Strings

Every morning, Paul walked past the foot of our bed and seized my big toe. He gently pulled and shook it. It was an odd form of affection. When he assumed I was sleeping, I would lift my leg and he continued to execute the early morning ritual. A somewhat silly, trivial, and unromantic act to most people, I sensed devotion and love "tugging" the stings of my heart. My turn to perform this gesture of devotion arose after Paul became bed ridden. I witnessed our kids doing the "tug" as they said goodnight to their dad during his last months. Years later, we find ourselves pulling one another's toes before shutting off the bedroom lights and saying, "Good night, love you!"

Some of the minor and trivial actions in life are taken for granted. They convey the most splendid and tender moments of our memories.

> Then the angel showed me the river of life—giving water, sparkling like crystal, flowing from the throne of God and the Lamb
>
> Revelation 22:1

Then he said to all, "If anyone wishes to come after me, he must deny himself and take up his cross daily and follow me. For whoever wishes to save his life will lose it, but whoever loses his life for my sake will save it. What profit is there for one to gain the whole world yet lose or forfeit himself?"

Luke9:23-24

Chapter 18

Within a split second of waking up each morning, my memory familiarized me of Paul's reoccurrence of cancer and of his death. A sickening, panic sensation overwhelmed my entire body. Depression and anxiety established a relentless battle crawling out of bed every morning and dealing with life.

With his death, Paul presented us a new calendar. Daily events, anniversaries, and memories coincided with the date Paul left us. January 1st didn't exist, only January 11th. From this date, our lives moved forward or traced backward in months and weeks. Time was only compared with that day.

Facing reality seemed impossible. I wanted to hide my head under the covers and never come out, ignore everything and everyone, and hope it all faded away. My energy-striped body ached with a nauseous sensation. I wept exceedingly. I had to wind myself up like a toy several times a day just to function for a fleeting period of time. I displayed a content facial expression only until the house was empty and I was finally alone. With the kids in school, I crept back in bed, dead to the world. Those secretive hours of sleep created a sheltered hideaway where I desired to reside. There was no requisite of thoughts or reflections. I desired to die.

Chels, Jake, Zach, and I severely grasp how depression and despair correlated with abuse, murders, and self-inflicted injuries, and even suicide. Depression wounds and devastates the body, impairs the mind, and tortures the soul. Random remarks suggested I or my kids should, "Just get over it," or "Go on with your life." Hints enlightened us that maybe we felt sorry for ourselves.

They didn't get it. When pain overwhelms your every thought and effort you put forth, life became intensely difficult. You only "exist."

"Existing" displays no glimmer of hope or flicker of light, just a vast dark void of nothingness. I never considered it an option to harm myself, but compelling thoughts did enter my mind. Death definitely would surpass suffering. Chels, Jake, and Zach kept me living for them. It was vital we supported and encouraged each other. We drew closer with invisible threads, helping each other to bear each new day and burden. I couldn't stomach having them lose another parent because of my own weakness and of my own selfishness.

Then the *"if's"* harassed me. *If* I had taken better care of Paul, *if* I would have recognized the cancer signs earlier, *if* I would have prayed harder, *if* we had caught the disease sooner, Paul would still be alive. Guilt constantly whispered in my thoughts that I rushed Paul's death. Guilt blamed everything on me. I should have tried harder to keep Paul alive.

Was this comparable to the "dark night of the soul" many saints experienced? Did God abandon me? Was I alone in my sorrow and distress? Life seemed obscure and heavy; my prayers seemed insignificant and pointless.

With the death of Paul, my light burned out. Everything I did was mechanical. I couldn't remember anything. My brain shut down. I repeated conversations over and over. My body and brain felt numb and foggy. I craved my sleeping pill before crawling out of bed in the mornings. I did not want to think about anything because "everything" was a strenuous chore. Where are you death?

Most of Paul's possessions remained how he last arranged them. His large assortment of miniature John Deere toy's stayed on their shelves in the hutch while his gun collection remained protected inside his gun case. His shirts, jackets, and suits resided in the bedroom closet with his cowboy boots for more than three years. Dust settled on them. They were not in the way. Paul's belongings clung to their rightful places. His scent lingered on them, and I wasn't prepared to discard them. His mixtures of fragrances flowed from the closet like a fresh bouquet of flowers. The leather, the Stetson, and even the body lotion used during his illness brought forth an exquisite flower garden of precious memories.

> Why are you so downcast, O my soul? Why do you sigh within me? Hope in God! For I shall again be thanking him, in the presence of my savior and my God.
>
> Psalm 43:5

Countless nights I would feel movement from Paul's side of the bed near my feet. My blanket would be gently pulled, or there would be a faint action as if someone were sitting down on the edge of the bed. It always awakened me.

Years earlier, our children often crawled into the king size bed with Paul and me after nightmares or a thunderstorm, but these latest perplexing incidents occurred after Paul left us. I assumed one of my kids was wriggling their way into my bed and didn't think twice.

After falling asleep once more, it happened again. A soft pull and a fragile movement from Paul's side of the bed woke me up. I let Zach settle down for his evening slumber.

It is a grave and dangerous transgression to summon or correspond with the spiritual world, especially with Satan. He transforms his light and trickery into beliefs we "desire to see" and "need to believe." Afterwards, the Living Truth is twisted to fit our wants. Satan portrays this toxic life extremely inviting, very entertaining, and much easier to follow. We then thirst and hunger for more of the destructive things in life.

If my family's experiences are from Satan himself, they backfired on him, for my faith in God has grown with each unforeseen occurrence. If they are truly from God, how blessed we are!

Zach was not sleeping on his dad's side of the bed. No one had been there!

> Behold, I tell you a mystery. We shall not all fall
> asleep, but we will all be changed.
>
> 1 Corinthians 15:51

Chapter 20

A year passed in haste and brought the ugly memory of Paul's seizure. The hands on the bedroom clock indicated the impending hour which altered our unpretentious lives. Nauseated and anxious, I awaited the dreaded minute. My mind replayed the enactment so many times. A deep, wounded soul struggled to console an intense broken heart.

At 8:27 a.m., an overwhelming peace engulfed me. This sensation flowed through my whole being. No earthly words could explain this phenomenon of eminence, love, and tranquility. It was not of this world. I silently lay in bed for an unknown amount of time, absorbing transcendent warmth and afraid to move, thinking this spiritual awareness might dissipate. I desired to remain in this realm of His divine ecstasy forever. Returning to the heartache of the other sphere seemed an unbearable thought. *This* is the real world.

I felt more comfortable and easy when this inexplicable event occurred a second time. My sorrow replenished into a loving warmth and heavenly peace at the precise time frame our family witnessed Paul's seizure a year earlier. Indescribable!

God's grace!

...but he said to me, "My grace is sufficient for you, for power is made perfect in weakness." I will rather boast most gladly of my weaknesses, in order that the power of Christ may dwell with me.

2 Corinthians 12:9

Chapter 21

Months after Paul passed away; I sensed a passionate beckoning from my soul to visit a local nursing home where my younger sister, Bobbi, is employed. She compassionately informed me of residents having no family support system or visitors. Some were dying alone.

Lorraine was one of these beautiful souls. Frequent meetings with her left us both feeling at peace. One morning's visit appeared unique. The day started out grueling for me. Depression wouldn't let me crawl out of bed, but a strong desire to see Lorraine persisted.

I walked into her room later in the morning. She gazed up at me and whispered, "Thank you, Lord." Removing her glasses, she spoke to me. "Thank you so much for coming."

"Are you having a bad day?" I questioned the exhausted appearance.

"No, I don't have bad days, just *a day*."

"Do you need a hug?" She presented a warm smile and gradually lifted her arms wide open. I wasn't aware she could move this much. In silence, I held her as she laid her head on my shoulder for several minutes.

"Your arm is so warm."

I smiled. "I love you and God does, too."

"Would you like some holy water?" I asked her reluctantly since she wasn't of the Catholic faith.

"No!"

I continued to hold her while she rubbed her forehead against my shoulder.

"What is *a day*?"

"A day today is, I want some holy water!" She astonished me with a tender smile.

"Are you sure?"

A soft "yes" came from her mouth.

"This water is like the water when you were baptized."

Lorraine allowed me to place some on her forehead in the sign of the cross as well as on her hands and wrist area, where the nails pierced Jesus. She did this by faith!

I once again fought depression by struggling with crawling out of bed on my next morning visit with Lorraine. God, being the perfect Father, blessed me with the "peace that surpasses all understanding."

Each time I encountered these blessings, I experience a bright flash in my head, sometimes with a popping sound. Other times I "feel/see" a phenomenon in my soul which is hard to explain in earthly terms. Warmth flooded my entire body after the burst of light. It is indefinable!

On a different occurrence with Lorraine, I found her lying in bed. She raised her head as far as she could from the headrest, scanning for something.

"Do you need holy water?" I timidly inquired.

She gently lay back down on her pillow. I placed small drops of liquid on her forehead and hands. Lorraine closed her eyes and embraced God's passion for her with peace, willingness, and perfect faith. From the extreme depths of her heart and soul, she experienced *His* love. Lorraine lay in bed absorbing the mystery of holy water. Only she and God knew what transpired during this sacred moment.

> Faith is the realization of what is hoped for and evidence of things not seen.
>
> Hebrews 11:1

Journal Two

Chapter 22

I promised Paul I would watch over his widowed mom, Arlene, several months before he passed away. My mother-in-law deemed a difficult time grieving and accepting the loss of her son. After Paul became bedridden, Arlene experienced denial and avoided seeing him. She always found excuses: soup to simmer, shopping, or something more vital.

I invited her numerous times to visit Paul at the farmhouse. She achieved a tough undertaking of coming out to celebrate three separate evening masses with Fr. Andrews and several of Paul's best friends, co-workers, and cousins.

Before the second hit with cancer, I often caught Paul in bed early, lying on his back and facing the ceiling. His legs fell horizontal and his hands clasped together as if in prayer. Another chance to tease him! "This is what you are going to look like when you are laying in your coffin. All you need are some flowers!

Paul conveyed his grin, and I kissed him goodnight while tucking the covers under his chin. "Quit fussing over me," he kindly advised me. Pre-cancer, Paul stopped at his mom's home at least once a day, whether to perform some honey-do-jobs or keep her company while watching a Nebraska football game. He was support for her. I sometimes considered her the "other woman," but she wasn't a threat to me. I loved her as I did her son.

She phoned Paul every week during his fourth stage of cancer. They conversed about events going on in her life and avoided the topic of his disease. She believed that if she didn't physically see Paul, then there wouldn't be anything wrong with him. Perhaps she only wanted to remember what Paul looked like years earlier, when he was stronger, healthier, and not resembling an old man.

I did not blame her for her actions. I understood. However, Arlene missed many blessings of telling Paul all of the wonderful things she needed him to know, such as how much she loved him and would miss him. She couldn't spend his final hours with him. Arlene and her son possibly didn't sense the need to carry out this action. Maybe it was a given. Love, at times, needs no words.

I remember Arlene's last phone call with Paul. She was busy in conversation and didn't perceive the events happening on the other end of the phone line. She kept chatting as if nothing was wrong.

Paul struggled to hold the receiver up to his ear without assistance. Weariness caused the communication almost unattainable as his head slanted heavily down toward his left shoulder. I sadly informed Arlene her son was too weak to speak with her.

Chels, Jake, Zach, and I used varied approaches dealing with Paul's impending death and actual passing. We each handled it at different times, in various ways, and with diverse degrees. Individual attention and concern for each of us became a demanding challenge every hour, night, and day.

I judged myself while drowning in grief. I failed Paul in promising him I would take care of his mom after his death. I visited with Arlene very few times during the months following his funeral. When I gazed at her, I saw Paul eyes and her sadness. It only added more weight to my own grief.

The kids felt physically and mentally shattered and beaten. No one could imagine the suffering they dealt with unless they themselves experienced this scenario as a child.

Focusing on school aided in ignoring the grief by placing their energy towards other things. Painful heartache thrust itself deeper into their wounded souls. For them, it became difficult listening to fellow classmates speak of their own dads. Conversations in the hallways were hard on my children on Monday mornings. The dialogue centered on what everyone experienced the day before with their "dads." It became a challenge for them to watch other fathers attend school events. Concentration during class was strenuous with lingering thoughts on their own dad.

The house seemed spiritually empty when they returned from school every afternoon. Daddy wasn't there anymore. A substantial weight placed itself on their tiny shoulders. They pictured themselves as orphans.

The extracurricular sports of football, baseball, and basketball lost their glossy luster after Paul passed away. What once seemed fun and enjoyable, with dad sitting in the bleachers, coaching the team, or practicing with them in the farm yard, now promoted stress and anxiety.

Deprivation of dad lingered around them. Life breathed a deficiency of priceless conversations with Dad. There was an absence of his suggestions of improving a baseball swing and his praises on a game played well. No more pictures could be taken with the boys and their father and coach.

Absenteeism from school became an immense culprit to defeat. I related with my kids when the desire to stay in bed immerged. Why go through the efforts of life? With time and patience, we received exceptional support from our medical family, educators, and staff that focused on working with our family in keeping up with overdue homework, tests, and tears.

Life was a worthless, never-ending nightmare. We constantly thought about Dad and the yet unsweetened memories that couldn't be erased from our minds. Thoughts of Paul became deeply engraved into the depths of every part of our lives. Every song, sound, and object in the house and on the farm brought dad back into our minds.

9-13-08

I had a dream about Dad last night. I was outside and I saw Dad just watching me. He was smiling. I ran up to him, and we hugged and kissed. I told my family that he was here. We could all see him. We enjoyed a whole weekend together. We spent a whole bunch of time together. On Monday, he dropped me off at the parking lot because I had to go to school. We hugged goodbye. I was almost in school when I looked and saw Dad disappear. I ran over there, no matter who saw me. I hugged the air and felt someone hug back.

When I told mom this she cried, and so did I. I told Mom I felt him right by the bed. I love you, Dad. You are my Cuzie! Bye!

(Cuzie, a nickname Jake and Paul gave each other)

12-20-08

Dear Cuzie or Dad,

I love you!! It is four days until Christmas. Thank you for my Christmas present. That was the best dream ever. We had a Christmas Concert already. I thought to myself that if I saw you I would run up to you and hug and kiss you. You are more important than public humiliation. In my dream, I was at the Christmas Concert singing, and I saw you so I ran up to you. You were wearing a white T-shirt and jeans. When you came towards me you had a flannel shirt over your white T-shirt. Everybody was staring at me hugging thin air. I was the only one that could see you. I hugged and kissed you. (In your clothes you also had a pliers and its holder.) I loved it when I hugged you. It was just like old times. It was the same body. I was feeling the same feeling I feel when I hug you. I also felt your nice, prickly beard against my cheek. Man, was that good. It lasted pretty long. Which was good. Then I woke up from my dream. I love You Cuzie, or Dad!!!!   ♥ ♥ ♥ ♥

With *ALL MY LOVE*,
Your Cuzie, Jake or Jacob

1-22-09

Dear Cuzie,

I love you, Dad. Two days ago in church when I was praying the Our Father with my hands raised up, I felt you push a finger on the palm of my hand. I snatched it and put it in my pocket. Whenever I miss you, I just take it out and rub it on my face and kiss it. (I'm doing it right now!!) I missed you today. I can't believe it has been over a year without you. I know right now you are saying, "I didn't go anywhere, I'm right here." But I just cannot see you. But you can see me. The Super Bowl is coming up. The Steelers and the Cardinals are playing. I love you. Gotta go! Bye!

With All my love,
Your Cuzie

1-30-09

Dear Cuzie,

I Love You! At Louie Kerkman's funeral when the Dwyers were singing "Daddy's Hand," I felt you grab my hand right after Mom grabbed my other hand. It was there for a long time. I wish you were here. My heart is empty without you. Pope John is doing good at sports. Nebraska is okay, too. I miss you. Chicklet is here with me when I am writing this. I love you and your beard. Say hi to everyone for me.

With All My Love,
Your Cuzie

"Chicklet" is a small stuffed yellow chicken Jake received for Easter many years earlier. Paul slept with it every night until he died.

> Hasten to answer me, Lord; for my spirit fails me. Do not hide your face from me, lest I become like those descending to the pit. In the morning let me hear of your mercy, for in you I trust. Show me the path I should walk, for I entrust my life to you.
>
> Psalm 143:7-8

Chapter 23

Unexplainable events occurred in our lives. The sunshine gleamed one quiet spring morning, several months after Paul's funeral. I stood beneath a maple tree beside our farm house. The young sapling shook itself off and showered me with drops from a recent overnight storm. I was amazed at how I became so drenched with the absence of a breeze.

Envision a loved one sitting on the edge of your bed. With your eyes closed you sense the movement; you know someone is there. Numerous times I underwent these sensations; someone sitting down, getting up from my bedside, and even lying next to me. These were not frightening encounters, they were uplifting blessings. Chelsea, Jake, and Zach also experienced such wonders.

Next time you lie in bed, close your eyes, and ask your husband or child to gently sit on your bedside. Without seeing, you can "believe."

> Then he said to Thomas, "Put your finger here and see my hands, and bring your hand and put it into my side, and do not be unbelieving, but believe." Thomas answered and said to him, "My Lord and my God!" Jesus said to him, "Have you come to believe because you have seen me? Blessed are those who have not seen and have believed."
>
> John 20:27-29

Chapter 24

As a devout Catholic and longtime resident of the local nursing home, Julius was often praying when I entered his room. We appreciated one another's company and our wonderful conversations and laughter. I sat with him during the last months. He unknowingly exposed many life-lessons.

Julius sensed how important water correlated to life. Holy water was often applied to his forehead and his hands, and he always seemed to thirst for more.

It had been several weeks since my last visit with him. Our family still dealt heavily with the loss of Paul. Julius's daughter phoned me one morning. Hurricane Ike kept her stranded in Texas.

Crying, she asked, "Could you sit with my dad?" She was unable to be by her father's bedside during his last days. She felt guilty. I said yes with much joy in my heart and devoted two peaceful hours to Julius. He also received the Anointing of the Sick from Father Andrews. "A day" for Julius concluded as a "blessed day!"

My next visit with Julius occurred on a stormy morning. While he slept, he prayed the Hail Mary with genuine devotion to our Blessed Mother and giving honor to her Son. After meditating on this prayer during his lifetime, it became engraved in his heart and soul. His love and trust for his spiritual mother left me amazed.

A loud thunder clapped and caused him to pray with more intensity.

Later when he awoke, Julius asked me, "Will you hold my hand and pray for me?"

I was honored to do this for him. I often prayed the Divine Mercy Chaplet for him as he slept. I experienced God's presence surrounding Julius. He sensed it too.

On one occasion, while praying the Chaplet for Julius, I stopped abruptly. My brain went totally blank.

"Julius, do you ever forget words to prayers you know by heart?"

He smiled and answered, "Yes!"

Julius always thanked me for spending time with him. One of those precious days I told him, "I love you."

"I love you, too."

At the age of ninety-nine years and ten months, Julius passed away peacefully October 10th, 2008.

> In the same way, the Spirit too comes to the aid of our weakness; for we do not know how to pray as we ought, but the Spirit itself intercedes with inexpressible groanings.
>
> Romans 8:26

> Have no anxiety at all, but in everything, by prayer and petition, with thanksgiving, make your requests known to God.
>
> Philippians 4:6

Chapter 25

I carried depression on my shoulders. God still abandoned me. He discarded all of us. Several of my friends were suffering the loss of their fathers or husbands and some dealt with breast cancer. I sensed their loss. I recognized their pain. Where is God? Where is He?

Sandy called one afternoon, October 12th, two days after Julius passed away.

"How are you?"

"Not good, I'm so sad."

"I know, I can feel your energy. Paul is all around you, and he loves you so very much." Then she asked, "Are you still visiting the nursing home?"

"Yes, I feel very peaceful going there."

"There is an elderly gentleman who wants to thank you for holding his hand and praying with him."

Julius!

I was stunned by Sandy's words. She had no knowledge or awareness of Julius.

"You are welcome Julius!"

> So we are always courageous, although we know that while we are at home in the body we are away from the Lord, for we walk by faith, not by sight. Yet we are courageous, and we would rather leave the body and go home to the Lord.
>
> 2 Corinthians 5:6-8

Chapter 26

Thanksgiving Day was nothing special. In the Mass homily, Father Andrews stated we all have much to be thankful. I left church early. I drove to the St. Boniface cemetery, where Paul was laid to rest. When I reached his abandoned grave, I collapsed down on my knees crying.

I screamed and yelled at Paul and at God. I pounded and pulverized the mound covering Paul's body repeatedly with my angry fists. I laid face down on the unfriendly dirt sobbing, I was so furious at both of them. How could they do this to me?

Married in our mid-thirties, we had a late start raising a family. With lots of love, we seemed eager to settle down and spend the rest of our lives together.

Every engaged Catholic couple is required to visit at least six months prior with their parish priest to prepare for their upcoming marriage. I felt hesitant in taking a mandatory questionnaire. Paul wasn't!

I remember Fr. Potts, Paul's parish priest and friend, with his hearty and robust laugh tell us we received a perfect score on our test. He never met an engaged couple so compatible for marriage!

Fr. Potts suggested we acquire a group picture of close friends taken at our wedding reception. He commented it would be nice to have in case something happened to one of them. As I write this book, two are missing from the photo: Fr. Potts and Paul!

Paul and I wanted the same things in life. We both prayed for each other. God answered our prayers, but he placed a veiled stipulation in his response. It seems we missed the tiny fine print at the bottom of his blessing. He didn't promise or give us a slight hint of how much time we had together.

The kids drove past the cemetery on their way home from church. They noticed me crying by their dad's grave site. After driving into the graveyard, Chelsea walked over to her dad's head stone. It was engraved with The Divine Mercy Image and "Jesus, I Trust in You." Wild sunflowers, similar to ones found in the pastures and the ditches, continuously adorn his burial site. With love and compassion, she gently grasped my arm and helped me up off the cold emotionless ground. Three kids took me home.

I am Blessed!

> At that time the disciples approached Jesus and said, "Who is the greatest in the kingdom of heaven?" He called a child over, placed it in their midst, and said, "Amen, I say to you, unless you turn and become like children, you will not enter the kingdom of heaven. Whoever humbles himself like this child is the greatest in the kingdom of heaven. And whoever receives one child such as this in my name receives me."
>
> Matthew 18:1-5

Chapter 27

The split second I ran out of our house with the door slamming shut behind me, the phone rang. I didn't hear the ringing. Totally in shock and disbelief, I headed for Elgin to inform Arlene of the horrible news of another son, her first born, passed away from a heart attack. My mind raced.

"How am I going to tell her Jim is gone? How am I going to tell her? She'll have a stroke or something!"

Jim didn't realize God desired him in Heaven within a few precious hours. He celebrated Eucharist and enjoyed a quiet Saturday evening meal with his wife, LuAnn. This was their *last supper!*

> Watch, therefore: you do not know when the lord of the house is coming, whether in the evening, or at midnight, or at cockcrow, or in the morning. May he not come suddenly and find you sleeping. What I say to you, I say to all: 'Watch!'"
>
> Mark 13:35-37

LuAnn sensed an extra happy Jim on the evening of his unexpected death. I often contemplate if Jim would have done anything different than what he did; I don't think so. He spent his final hours with his two loves, Jesus and LuAnn. How awesome!

LuAnn understood Jim's heart was getting weaker. Trips by ambulance and office visits became more frequent than usual. Clueless to the life changing events to befall her in the twilight of November 29th, 2008, LuAnn wasn't prepared.

They both had just gotten home. Jim went down the basement steps when LuAnn perceived a loud thump. She found her husband collapsed at the bottom of the stairs. His face and lips displayed purple and bluish colors from lack of oxygen.

"Don't leave me, please, don't leave me!" she pleaded.

She trembled as she knelt by Jim's side. LuAnn started CPR compressions once she regained her senses and acknowledged the events materializing.

The EMT's resuscitated Jim several times without success. On three occasions, they sent LuAnn on an errand. She suspects they kept her away for a purpose, but she wanted to be at her husband's side. The first task required that she compiled a list of prescription medicines Jim took. The second chore she needed to check on her niece who called the rescue unit earlier.

Standing on the stairs a third time provided her with an unseen, veiled blessing. LuAnn, with tears in her eyes described her spiritual experience as, "I felt a light brush of air, a soft breeze, like a feather gently going across my face and continuing up the stairs. I knew it was Jim leaving me. I knew in my heart it was him, but I didn't want to admit it.

"When the time came, I wasn't ready to let Jim go, but I knew the time was coming. Every time I go down those stairs now, I visualize Jim laying there. The memories and emotions flood back to me. Nothing is ever set on that spot. It is 'sacred ground.'

"I always believed I would be the one who would save Jim. I took classes, and I knew what to do. I could save him." LuAnn made God smile. *He* had other plans.

After returning home hours later, tired and still in shock, Jake informed me Sandy called the exact time I left the house earlier. I immediately returned her phone call.

"Hi Sandy,"

"Hi Karen, how are you?"

"Not good, Paul's brother just died."

"I know."

"How do you know?"

"Because I can see a man's figure with Paul, the image is not complete. He doesn't know he is dead yet."

"That's Jim!"

"I was meditating, and I got Paul. Paul is such a sweet spirit. He had urgency about him. Call Karen! Call Karen! My dad was there, too. Tell Karen, "I'm there! I'm there! I'm there! Paul knew Jim was going to die. They are together now."

A gentle person, Jim filled our lives with love and with laughter. Losing him became another dreadful jolt to our family. The two weeks Paul and I resided at the Omaha hospital; Jim's daily visits brought support and concern for his baby brother and teasing me of my terrible parking skills in the hospital parking lots.

While Paul lay in his bed at home with cancer, Jim shared something amazing with his brother. "Paul, I wish I could give up my life for you and take your place, cancer and all. LuAnn and I don't have any kids. Your kids need you."

Only God knew what would transpire nine short months later.

With a tearful evening of stories, LuAnn shared more memories of Jim with me.

"One night shortly after his death, I was in bed. I felt the sensation like I was being tucked in by him. Jim always tucked the covers behind my back, so the cold wouldn't get in. I was afraid to move, the feeling would go away. I also felt like he was holding me, like his arm was over me like he used to do. I was happy and at peace. I felt he was letting me know everything will be okay."

LuAnn and Jim had a blessed marriage. They were not blessed with children, but they were graced with each other. Priceless! They recognized the value of genuine love and respect for each other. God was priority in their union. He was the foremost nourishment for their healthy marriage.

When Jim left us, he still gave. He donated parts of his body, eyes, skin and longer bones, so someone else would be blessed.

Arlene was passionate about her faith and trusted in God's will completely. She informed me years later in the nursing home that the year both her sons died was the hardest time in her life. She never shed a tear for her husband Eddie or either of her sons. She took her leaden crosses, accepted them, and never doubted his love for her. She carried the pain inside her soul. Consequently, her tiny frame became frailer each day, and her mental state declined. The cross became too heavy. Soon after Jim's death, she became diagnosed with adult failure to thrive.

She was slowly dying from a broken heart.

When assisting Jim's wife, LuAnn, prepare funeral arrangements, one of Paul and Jim's sisters came into the living room and sat down on the couch. She had a puzzled look on her face.

"I could swear I felt someone sit on the edge of my bed early this morning, but no one was there!"

I never mentioned the events I experienced the past nine months to my sister-in-law. I now heard proof. I wasn't going crazy. It does happen to other people.

One phone call, Sandy commented, "I wish people wouldn't say their loved ones are dead. They're not dead. They're changed!"

During another phone call, Sandy informed me she kept hearing Paul say, "Zach, Zach, baseball, baseball over and over again," and "whatever he decides, it's okay." I spoke to Zach about what Sandy conveyed to me.

It was only March 9th. I hadn't been in the baseball mindset since last year's season. I questioned Zach if he thought about playing. He grew serious. The boys at school were trying to persuade him into playing, but he didn't want to since he missed dad's coaching.

Paul aided the Jr. Pee Wee and Pee Wee teams for several years with his friend Billy Pelster. Co-volunteer coaching duties and the talents of the young boys led the teams to excel at games and tournaments.

"Zach, do what you feel happiest with."

The decision was made. He proudly wore a part of Dad out on third base and on the pitcher's mound: Paul's ancient, well broken in baseball glove, "the Legend!"

The unexplainable twinkling between awake and asleep, I experience the phenomenal blessings of someone sitting on my bed.

On one distinctive occurrence, I detected someone sit on the edge of my bed, but this time I noticed additional movement. The activity seemed identical to little "children" jumping up and down and all around me, as if Chelsea, Jake, and Zach played on my bed, jumping, but much more delicate.

Another time as I lay on my side in bed not thinking of anything in particular, from one direction energy flowed through my torso between my shoulders and my waist. A gentle force entered and left, repeating itself three or four times. This sensation seemed different from other times "the spirit" overcame me. Total peace!

Only God knows!

3-15-09

Dear Cuzie,

I love you. Two days ago I really missed you, and I was crying because you were the only one who understood me and the only one I could talk to. I was up with Mom until 11:00 p.m. Then Mom had to pick up Chelsea from a party. After mom left, I was still crying, but then all of a sudden peace flowed through my veins and through my body. It was the Holy Spirit. It calmed me down, and then I fell right asleep. I love you, Dad. Cuzie!! I wish I and the whole family can see you more.

With all my love,
Your Cuzie, Jake

Come now, you who say, "Today or tomorrow we will go into such and such a town, spend a year there doing business, and make a profit"— you have no idea what your life will be like tomorrow. You are a puff of smoke that appears briefly and then disappears.

James 4:13-15

No one has greater love than this, to lay down one's life for one's friends.

John 15:13

Chapter 28

My entire body hurt from depression. I pleaded, *"Father, please let the Holy Spirit come to me."* A tsunami of peace flowed through me as I lay in bed. A wave of stillness and warmth engulfed all of my aching.

I acquired a fervent internal desire to pray the Divine Mercy Chaplet. With each supplication, tranquility continued to increase in vigor and to surge with intensity. My "being" became inadequate for the full extent of his divine gift. I craved this blessing and as it increased in strength, I sensed a need to blackout. What really amazed me was that I couldn't feel my body.

With my hands and legs numb, I tried moving and awaited the dreaded "pins and needles" effect. However, I didn't suffer it, for my limbs were not asleep.

My physical form was incapable of enduring the graces God graciously bestowed upon me. My spiritual soul seized every droplet of His love and peace. It wasn't an amazing dream but an unbelievable reality.

In the stillness I heard, *"I love you, my daughter."*

> Have no anxiety at all, but in everything, by prayer and petition, with thanksgiving, make your requests known to God. Then the peace of God that surpasses all understanding will guard your hearts and minds in Christ Jesus.
>
> Philippians 4:6-7

If you then, who are wicked, know how to give good gifts to your children, how much more will the Father in heaven give the holy Spirit to those who ask him?

Luke 11:13

Journal Three

Chapter 29

January 24, 2009

S andy called from the east coast this afternoon. "How are you?" she asked.

"I'm okay."

"Paul is telling me you are having a hard time getting out of bed." I started crying. My secret became revealed. Paul exposed a shameful hidden behavior. I couldn't keep the tears from flowing. *How does Sandy know this stuff?*

Later in our conversation, I confided about an earlier miscarriage soon after Chelsea's birth. We named our baby soul, Amy Elizabeth, which means "Beloved" and "Consecrated to God."

We also assumed Jake had been a twin because of an extra amniotic sac alongside Jake's. Chelsea and Jacob Robert had the awesome idea of naming their brother Robbie Jacob.

"Finally, finally you are talking about it! I've been waiting, and I didn't want to ask if you had a miscarriage or something. Yes, I have been seeing two little spirits beside Paul, always with him. I see them often sitting on your bed, a girl and a boy!" She continued, "Paul loves you so much!"

Was this a connection to when I felt someone jumping on the bed beside me, as if it were my kids but on more of a delicate, mystical level?

"I could have been a better wife, and when Paul was dying I could have been more helpful," I said as tears streamed down my face.

"You did great! Paul is with you. He is energy, and energy never loses or goes away; it changes to something else."

Still today, I catch myself immerged deep in profound sadness. Physical vigor is exhausting while my legs and arms lose their strength and will power. They hold the quality of wet noodles. A trodden soul melts. I anticipate crumbling to the floor in a big heap of sadness. I don't surrender. I continue standing and walking while praying for graces to conquer sporadic minutes of hopelessness. I offer the suffering up to God. Looking back at all of the anxiety and apprehension my family underwent, we endured many blessings by the grace of God.

> They that hope in the LORD will renew their strength, they will soar as with eagles' wings; They will run and not grow weary, walk and not grow faint.
>
> Isaiah 40:31

Chapter 30

February 1, 2009

S andy called this morning. Paul came to her while she meditated. He told her, "I am closest to Karen when she is in church."

She continued, "At night when you go to bed, Paul has his arms around you."

"Why did God bless me with you and being able to hear messages from Paul?"

"Don't use your energy to figure it out, use your energy to be thankful and have gratitude."

February 3rd, 2009

"Paul let me know you went back to bed again today," Sandy revealed to me. I did crawl back into bed. I still couldn't deal with life.

February 4th, 2009

I yearned to sneak back into bed after the kids left for school, but I didn't. Paul would convey my little secret to Sandy. I struggled to keep myself busy the remainder of the day. These phone calls were part of the support system in keeping me out of bed and helping fight against depression.

Paul perceived my plans. I didn't want him to tattle on me again!

> For there is nothing hidden that will not become visible, and nothing secret that will not be known and come to light.
>
> Luke 8:17

Chapter 31

Sandy and I got close that year. Our phone calls consisted of exuberant laughing, breathtaking stories, and occasional cleansing tears. Time flew during our chats. She still never ceases to astonish me with her words.

"You better feed Zach. He's hungry." Sandy informed me laughing.

"What did you say?"

"Zach's hungry. Paul told me he was hungry."

She was oblivious of Zach's soundless attempts to get me off the phone. He tried displaying a comically famished facial expression and clasping his stomach from hunger pangs. Three times I silently waved him out of my bedroom, and three times he returned, starving to death.

I shared with Zach the latest incident revealing proof his dad was still with us.

"I always knew Mom, but you always get all 'huggy and stuff!'"

Shortly after that day, Zach needed to talk to me one night after I got home from a meeting.

"I saw black figures four times in different rooms of the house tonight." he whispered, terrified. We prayed and sprinkled holy water throughout the rooms. I asked

Zach to sing a Latin song he memorized during mass. He then felt safe and sheltered.

Another occasion led Zach to inform me he was witnessing another black figure. This form happened to be peeking over the corner of the buffet in the living room as we talked in the parlor.

After a Divine Mercy Holy Hour at the church, Jake claimed to have caught a glimpse of a white, misty figure walking up by the altar. He also noticed them in our home. I cannot tell the boys it is their imagination. I believe them!

I trust my children when they tell me their farfetched stories. Just because others may not accept what Chels, Jake, Zach, and I experience, doesn't mean it did not happen.

We are blessed even with the scary figures. The understanding may not be clear, but we remain aware of the veiled realm hiding beside, behind, and around us.

I worried about my kids. Each dealt with their individual moments of tears and desolation. It hadn't even been a year since Paul passed away when Chelsea shocked me with an unforgettable testimony which broke my heart: *"Mom, I can't remember what Dad sounded like. I can't remember his voice or his laugh."*

Chelsea also revealed the stories of what she went through a couple years after her dad's death. I hadn't a clue to some of her concealed desperation and misery.

I apologized to her for several unaware events transpiring in her life. While I dealt with my mother-in-laws, the boys' and my grief, Chelsea hid her heartache behind her big smile. Her goal was to protect me from additional anxiety and stress. At times, she cried, but held most of the pain in to keep me from worrying. I became blinded and overwhelmed with life. I remember questioning her one day why Paul's death didn't give her much sadness. She smiled and told me everything was okay.

Chelsea also recalls one night where I was bawling in the darkness of my bedroom. Opening the oak door, she questioned, "Mom, are you okay?"

In the midst of all my emotions, I got mad at her. "Why aren't you ever sad? Don't you miss Dad?"

The words pierced my daughter, but she understood that I was in grief. She closed the door behind her and allowed me to be alone. She never held the words against me or brought them up.

I am sorry, Chelsea.

Jake was angry. He missed Dad, and he cared less about anything. He hated life and couldn't wait to die.

On one account, Jake angrily tore up a thick magazine into tiny pieces, threw them into the air, and said with bitterness, "*This is my heart!*"

Jake's approach to his dad's passing included putting all his energy into basketball.

Zach did the opposite. Missing Daddy erased the joy of playing junior high and high school sports games. His happiness instead evolved into casual, stress free games after school and on weekends with his brother and friends. God steered Zach away from sports and onto a new route in *his* direction!

I became apprehensive about Zach. He seemed overly stressed in dealing with the loss of his dad. Zach declined to discuss his father. He hated life, himself, and his dad. He believed we didn't love him.

He left Mass early one Saturday evening. After failed and repeated attempts to pry into Zach's heart, it finally cracked open a little. He cried for two long, exhausting days and felt much better after. I suspected we were getting a handle on his grief. I was wrong.

I prayed Zach would dream about an angel, Dad, or something to help his weary spirit. Several nights later he visualized one and described it in my journal:

> Zach here. I had a good dream about an angel. It appeared in a white light. It had huge wings. His garment was full of gems of colors I couldn't explain except for orange. We looked at each other for a while. Then he went away in a white light with a little smile.

Things got worse. Zach showed obvious signs of depression. At first he didn't want to discuss issues. He asked me to drive him out to the parish cemetery three or four times in one day to be with his dad, one time while raining.

Eleven-year-old Zach exhibited anger, betrayal, and hate towards Paul whom he now disowned.

"Dad should have said he was sorry for dying and abandoning me!" he said furiously.

He began missing school, days and weeks at a time. Every word I spoke to him was in vain. Everything I done for him was useless.

He screamed at me, *"You don't understand!"* Zach attempted to pull his hair out by the fistfuls. He had the needs to hit something and to harm himself. I saw his anger intensify beyond his control. Talking to him didn't help. He took my advice as "tearing him down." Comments consisted of "Dad would put me up instead of down."

I wasn't a perfect mom. I did the best I knew how to. Paul's death completely destroyed Zach's heart. He was incapable of hearing the compliments, and if he did, they were taken the wrong way.

One of our friends suggested getting him something to beat on. I found an old block of wood from the old tractor shed. With no mercy on the wood or the hammer, Zach spelled *Paul* with a handful of nails. He took his frustrations out as he pounded, screamed, sobbed, and yelled at his dad and God, "Why? Why? Why?" Many of these episodes lasted later than one o'clock in the morning.

Chelsea couldn't endure watching her baby brother act in this repulsive manner. She wept. My daughter begged me to do whatever it took to make him stop. There was nothing I could do.

Zoloft eased some, but not all, of his inner frustrations. His anger snowballed and so did his homework. Absenteeism from school escalated. I faced difficult challenges getting him out of bed, off the couch, and one time off the farm driveway. We sought different medicines for Zach, but nothing repaired his heart.

He slept. His entire body ached. Zach covered his head with his blanket or pillow and blocked out the world and all of its pain. I struggled to get him back into life. He became bigger and stronger when anger exposed itself. He would get his frustrations from his dad out by screaming and yelling angrily at me. Not once did he ever hit or abuse me. I sensed he retained that part of him on the inside, right below the stinging surface. He was hurting so immensely, and I couldn't make the pain go away. I was failing as a mom.

I understood what he felt because I myself still existed there.

Thoughts were not straight. Paranoia became normal because Zach believed we rallied against him. He desired to get rid of the pain in any way possible.

He wanted to harm himself. Zach informed me he tried to break into the locked gun cabinet. Extreme courage and God's grace helped him reveal his failed plan. He bore considerable amounts of anger and despair to finally cry out for help before becoming too late.

I immediately hid all of Paul's rifles and got them off the farm as soon as I could. Concern and uneasiness filled my days. Should I leave Zach alone for any length of time? With his state of mind, I remained on "high" alert every second of the day and night.

I wanted to shake him hard by the shoulders and tell him to *"knock it off."* The pressure was becoming too much. I continued to ride on this miserable merry-go-round with him.

I never imagined the guns Paul cleaned and polished diligently before he died would be used by our youngest son to attempt an unsuitable action. My trust in *God* appeared shaky. Why did *he* dislike us so much? Couldn't we have one good day?

I prayed, "*God, why does Zach have to go through this? He's only eleven. He's a baby! God, give it to me instead, I'll handle it. I'll keep busy. Please let Zach be happy again.*"

I received a phone call from Sandy. She knew events were in progress but not knowing the details. I filled her in on Zach being depressed about his dad.

"Wood, I see wood." Sandy commented.

I explained the block of wood and the hammer.

Zach had various issues in trying to overcome grief. Comments like, "I'm not taking those pills, it isn't the real me," and "with the counselors I can say what they want to hear," proved that in Zach's eyes, they were a waste of time. When put on depression medicines, he gradually weaned himself off without telling me. I believed the trips to Norfolk for therapy were productive.

The first three years appeared the toughest for Zach. The anniversary of his dad's death was always the hardest time of the year. With his emotions on a roller coaster, we couldn't predict what each day would bring. I knew it was vital that he straightened out his life before he masked these difficult issues with smoking, drinking, drugs, and promiscuity.

I pushed him to engage in the school's football and basketball teams. I thought they would free his mind. However, an injured swollen knee and surgery didn't help his morale at all. Zach's heart remained empty and broken. His continued long journey consisting of cutting and wounding alternatives which broke our family's spirit and we do not speak of today.

We needed a remedy.

Zach finally leaned on *the* cross.

The pills, the counseling, the sports, or any of the other heart-breaking routes taken were not the solution. It was *God*. Zach attended J.C. (Jesus Christ) Camps and Quest retreats. He discovered himself and the immense consuming love God showered on him, *the peace that surpasses all understanding!*

We were blind by earthly cures. The remedy surrounded us the entire time.

Jesus said to St. Faustina:

> *My daughter, I want to teach you about spiritual warfare. Never trust in yourself, but abandon yourself totally to My will. In desolation, darkness and various doubts, have recourse to Me and to your spiritual director. He will always answer you in My name. Do not bargain with any temptation; lock yourself immediately in My Heart and, at the first opportunity, reveal the temptation to the confessor. Put your self-love in the last place, so that it does not taint your deeds. Bear with yourself with great patience. Do not neglect interior mortifications. Always justify to yourself the opinions of your superiors and of your confessor. Shun murmurs like a plague. Let all act as they like; you are to act as I want you to....If someone causes you trouble, think what good you can do for the person who caused you to suffer. Do not pour out your feelings. Be silent when you are rebuked. Do not ask everyone's opinion, but only the opinion of your confessor; be as frank and simple as a child with him. Do not become discouraged by ingratitude. Do not examine with curiosity the roads down which I lead you.*

When boredom and discouragement beat against your heart, run away from yourself and hide in My heart. Do not fear struggle; courage itself often intimidates temptations, and they dare not attack us. Always fight with the deep conviction that I am with you. Do not be guided by feeling, because it is not always under your control; but all merit lies in the will. Always depend upon your superiors, even in the smallest things. I will not delude you with prospects of peace and consolations; on the contrary prepare for great battles. Know that you are now on a great stage where all heaven and earth are watching you. Fight like a knight, so that I can reward you. Do not be unduly fearful, because you are not alone. (1760)

You are united to me; fear nothing. But know, my child, that Satan hates you; he hates every soul, but he burns with a particular hatred for you, because you have snatched so many souls from his dominion (412). The glory of the Divine Mercy is resounding, even now, in spite of the efforts of its enemies, and of Satan himself, who has a great hatred for God's mercy. This work will snatch a great number of souls from him, and that is why the spirit of darkness sometimes tempts good people violently, so that they may hinder the work (1659).

For you say, 'I am rich and affluent and have no need of anything' and yet do not realize that you are wretched, pitiable, poor, blind, and naked.

Revelation 3:17

Chapter 32

"Who dumped cereal in the hamper?" I yelled unwaveringly at the kids from our bathroom. The sizable hamper contained a mixture of dirty clothes and alphabet cereal. Immediately, I received a persistent reply from one innocent victim of whom the guilty party was. I shook my head in disbelief. Life remained too short to sweat the small stuff.

An early breakfast escapade left Zach spilling a bowl, milk and cereal on his lap. He decided the laundry hamper would be the ideal hideaway to dispose of all lingering evidence, hoping I wouldn't find the mess. But, in his improper choice, a genuine blessing accrued several minutes later.

As I continued sorting and pulling out clothes needing to be washed, I stopped. On one of the garments three breakfast cereal pieces spelled out in capital letters: *D–A–D!*

I couldn't believe what I was looking at! I needed confirmation to what came into view and attained Chelsea's attention quickly.

"Mom, it spells out "dad"!" She said with her widest grin and optimistic eyes.

We commenced to show her two younger brothers this phenomenon and took several photos of it.

After an abundant amount of tossing clothes back and forth in the hamper, this word came into view. No one manipulated their arrangement. The letters formed a cherished blessing, materialized from a child's secretive endeavor.

I have three awesome, compassionate children! They are far from perfect. They disagree, have messy bedrooms, love junk food, and they're kids! However, they were given a gift: the ability to actually listen deep into their hearts. With much trauma in such a short time, they endured a worldly hell. They survived and are stronger and wiser for it.

For in losing a life they respect life more.

The kids highly honored their daddy on Mother's Day a year after Paul left us. Chelsea started the morning by gifting me with a beautiful "family" frame and a candle. Four years earlier on Mother's Day, Paul surprised me with a lilac bush. Chelsea knew the scent of lilacs brought memories and Paul back, if only for a second in time.

Later in the day, Zach stood me in the middle of our living room. *When The Stars Go Blue* by Tim McGraw played off a CD while Zach danced with me. Of course, I cried over all of this!

Jake completed the day. I heard boots, Paul's boots walking around the house. I shut my eyes and soaked in the sounds and memories as Jake walked through the house making Paul alive again.

The day ended beautiful especially when Chels, Jake, and Zach appeared in my bedroom carrying a large brownie adorned with one candle for me. Children are a true blessing from God!

> "See that you do not despise one of these little ones, for I say to you that their angels in heaven always look upon the face of my heavenly Father."

Matthew 18:10

Chapter 33

A surprise call from the East coast delivered a message of peace one challenging Sunday morning. New unexpected forms of stress developed as the days progressed into weeks. With respect to family members, details will again be held in confidence.

I confided in Sandy concerning the latest burden on my shoulders. She continually senses when I require a dousing of positive reinforcement.

"Paul knows what is going on….I keep seeing hands open and outward together."

"I don't understand what your words mean," I replied.

Later in the afternoon, I knelt down beside my bed to pray. In astonishment, I raised my eyes to witness Sandy's mystifying words. On the bedroom wall hung "Come unto Me." It held my full attention. After falling in love with this art piece by Joann Reed at our church auction, I purchased this picture. I needed it in my home.

The print is composed of Jesus' hands open and extending forward. In doing so, his actions desire us to come to him.

I knelt on my knees in awe!

> "Come to me, all you who labor and are burdened, and I will give you rest."

> Matthew 11:28

Journal Four

Chapter 34

The environment left an atmosphere of safety on the wrap-around porch of our old farm house as I witnessed the evening sky from our swing. The land and the dust settled down for the night. The only activities were from our cats. Purring, Linus, Minka, and Smokie relished rubbing their arched backs against our legs and sometimes ended up lounging on our laps.

The "creak" of the metal swing soothed me while I swayed back and forth on this tranquil evening. Heavy thoughts remained on our miscarried baby, Amy Elizabeth, and of Paul. The day before had been yet another anniversary of a D&C performed in Norfolk many years earlier. Even though this child had been only weeks conceived, I felt a tremendous loss and suffered unimaginable sorrow after the surgery. I cried for months. The event didn't seem to disturb Paul's heart in the least.

Somewhat annoyed with his nonchalant manner, I questioned him on numerous accounts.

"How come you don't cry? Don't you care we lost a baby? Why don't you show some kind of emotion?"

Paul would shrug his shoulders and never provided me with a hoped-for answer.

One late afternoon, months after my surgery, Paul trudged into our house with a sorrowful expression.

He held me tight, wept on my shoulder, and conveyed how the pain from the loss of baby Amy suddenly overwhelmed him. The grief-stricken tears sought out the significant quest of healing and cleansing a shattered heart.

Years later when Paul's father passed away, I questioned him, "Why don't you ever go out to the cemetery and visit your dad?"

With a simple and truthful answer he replied, "He's not out there." I said no more for I understood.

I continued reminiscing on the porch swing concerning life's losses. The night sky embraced several clouds and a dazzling moon. I ached to be with Paul and to meet my Amy and glanced up at the heavens. A cloud formed an outline of a flawless "half" heart shape. *That cloud shape is a half heart, wouldn't it be weird if the other half filled in a full heart?*

And it did! The clouds fashioned an impeccable, picture-perfect heart. Light reflecting from the moon streamed through the aperture.

"Mom, that's a perfect heart!" Chelsea passionately spoke. She sprinted into the house to retrieve her camera from the living room buffet. The dimness of the evening produced a vacant photo but did not cause us disappointment. Chels and I have faith in what we saw, one more of *his* many blessings.

> The heavens declare the glory of God, and the firmament proclaims his handiwork.
>
> Psalm 19:1

Then we who are alive, who are left, will be caught up together with them in the clouds to meet the Lord in the air, thus we will shall always be with the Lord.

1 Thessalonians 4:17

Chapter 35

Chels, Jake, and Zach miss their dad each day and every night, longing to tell him of the events in their life. Occasions like being part of the basketball varsity team, portraying the "Mad Hatter" for a play, becoming part of the Student Council, or making the High Honor Roll. These are a small quantity of life's treasures which need to be shared with your dad. Our kids missed his "Goodnight! Love ya! See you in the morning!" and "Don't let the bed bugs bite!" shouts from the bottom of the aged worn-out oak staircase.

Just moments before, Paul bestowed on them a "Dad" hug. A goodnight kiss on their cheek and a tousling of hair ended their day, and they scrambled up the wooden steps. On numerous occasions, one or sometimes all three siblings would trace down the stairs. A habitual well-worn excuse brought them back into our living room, either for a final drink of water, a second hug, or simply alone time with dad in his recliner.

These young kids no longer have the chance to see their daddy early in the mornings before him heading out to do farm chores or heading out to Tintern. Memories of dad sipping hot coffee at the kitchen table and greeting them with a "Mornin'!" and a grin still linger in their minds. We miss the *clop clop* resonating off Paul's boots in the early, crisp silence.

Easter Sunday had lost memories after Paul left. We never received an answer whether Paul simply forgot or was playing along for the kids' sake. The Easter Bunny never failed to leave a surprise in Paul's worn out cowboy boots that morning. Paul proceeded to be startled when his toes discovered yet another brightly colored egg as his pulled on his boots.

With their dad absent, Zach and Jake didn't have a choice but to sacrifice many father and son occasions their friends may take for granted, such as driving John Deere tractors, checking pivots, or going fishing together. The "personal talks" only a dad would understand wouldn't occur. Moms, no matter how hard we try, can never take the place of a father. God created fathers for extraordinary motives!

Walking down the long church aisle with their dad is what many girls fantasize about. It is an important part of the "Cinderella Story" dream wedding. Hopefully all parents pray the man their "baby girl" falls in love with imitates the same devotion and adoration for their daughter as her daddy did. This sentimental stroll along with the opportunity for the "father-daughter" dance will never exist for Chelsea.

The gift of "a scent" is taken for granted; it often goes unnoticed until a loved one leaves us and then is recognized amongst clothing and possessions. One of many blessings Chels, Jake, and Zach received was in recognizing Paul's personal scents. They generated countless treasured memories simply by acknowledging and appreciating such blessings. Whenever the farming scents of cattle, grease and oil, and leather enter their noses, they detect their dad's presence nearby. However, it doesn't replace their father. Paul's "Stetson" cologne was sprinkled countless times on bed pillows, blankets, and stuffed toys merely to have dad near. Mingled with warm tears it aided all of us at some point into the realm of no pain; sleep.

On one occasion, I just returned home from an evening Pope John volleyball game. Zachary had experienced an extremely difficult day missing his dad. He was waiting for me outside by the garage.

Our youngest wore an enormous grin, and his eyes sparkled with complete untainted joy. His sadness had dissipated. While shooting hoops on the pavement, he detected a slight "scent of dad" lingering near the garage. He noticed the aroma becoming stronger the closer he moved to this particular area. The fragrance of "Daddy" was so undeniable. Zach understood his father's presence.

If and when we open our eyes and our hearts we are able to unearth God's modest and humble blessings *he* bestows on us no matter how small.

> Blessed are they who mourn, for they will be comforted.
>
> Matthew 5:4

Chapter 36

Jake decided to stay home instead of attending one of Chelsea's volleyball games with me. Walking into the house after the game, Jake informed me of an uncontrollable urge to pray he experienced while completing his homework. Jake kept pushing this strong sensation away. The impulse remained persistent.

After a period of uncertainty and apprehension, Jake resolved to pray. He didn't know who or what his prayers his were intended for, but realized someone needed his help. I advised that he will most likely never know. This turned out to be an incorrect statement.

Early the next morning, we learned upsetting news that an Eischeid family member fell and hit her head traumatically at work. She had been life-flighted and admitted to an Omaha hospital during the same time frame as my son's inner calling to pray. Jake understood his petitions to be crucial.

God answered Jake's prayers!

(To Daddy)   10-22-09

Last night I had a dream about you, Dad. Well, you were coaching Zach's team for baseball with Billy Pelster, I was doing the book with Alex. When the game was over, everybody sat on the bench, and I sat by you and leaned against you with relaxation. It felt just like you, Dad. I miss you. Sandy came the other day. It was fun. She liked cats especially all of them. She was funny and spiritual. Got to go, Bye! I love you.

With All My Love,
Jake Eischeid

While enjoying a conversation with Sandy, old memories surfaced of when Paul and I dated and how I missed him before he even left my house in Norfolk. I started crying.

"It's a blessing to have only one day of this feeling," Sandy said, "Did you hear what I just said, *'it's a blessing to have only one day of this feeling.'* Paul just told me that!"

Sandy phoned a couple days after one of Paul's uncles passed away. She wanted to share words Paul was revealing with her at the exact moment.

"Being with someone who is dying is so very important. When you had your kids, Paul was completely *'there,'* all body and spirit waiting for the birth of your kids. You were also completely *'there'*-completely! Birth is the same as death. They both are a birth. It is so important to be with the dying, to be *'there'* for them. Paul is with you when you go to the nursing home. He loves you so much!"

> So let us confidently approach the throne of grace to receive mercy and to find grace for timely help.
>
> Hebrews 5:16

166

Chapter 37

Many times, we as parents get wrapped up in friendly conversations that entice us at school games and events. I occasionally find myself remembering more of these chats than of my child's game.

On this one particular volleyball match, I participated in a deep conversation with a close friend, Michele. The discussion immersed into different aspects of our lives. The games continued but on a separate, lower plane of awareness.

My big toe experienced a sudden sturdy yank. The quick pull startled me, prompting me of past memories of Paul tugging my toe every morning. As my thoughts and beliefs stirred, I became aware and attentive to a spiritual and unseen environment.

Are we mindful of a mystical life that continually surrounds us? Do we acknowledge the "veiled" realm or do we prefer to use our lower level of awareness? Possibly, we feel threatened of its existence and therefore ignore it.

Chelsea, Jake, Zach, and I celebrated Holy Mass one Saturday evening at our home parish. Like all of us at times, Chelsea's mind started to wander. A "certain boy" became the center of her attention, rather than what was transpiring in front of her. Near the time of the Eucharistic consecration, Chelsea experienced a chill go up her spine.

"Pay attention!" an inner voice conveyed. These words captured her complete attentiveness towards her surroundings, of another world and dimension, unseen, and existing permanently around her.

Jesus said to St. Faustina:

> Write for the benefit of religious souls that it delights Me to come to their hearts in Holy Communion. But if there is anyone else in such a heart, I cannot bear it and quickly leave that heart, taking with Me all the gifts and graces I have prepared for the soul. And the soul does not even notice My going. After some time, inner emptiness and dissatisfaction will come to her attention. Oh, if only she would turn to Me then, I would help her to cleanse her heart, and I would fulfil everything in her soul; but without her knowledge and consent, I cannot be the Master of her heart. (1683)
>
> I desire to unite Myself to human souls, Know, My daughter, that when I come to a human heart in Holy Communion, My hands are full of all kinds of graces which I want to give to the soul. But souls do not even pay any attention to Me; they leave Me to Myself and busy themselves with other things...They treat Me as a dead object. (1385)
>
> I saw how unwillingly the Lord Jesus came to certain souls in Holy Communion. And He spoke these words to me: I enter into certain hearts as into a second Passion. (1598)

Chelsea and Jake attended a JC Camp out at Tintern. Chelsea volunteered to present a speech on peer pressure, which made her nervous since some of her classmates sat in the crowd.

As she stood by the office area waiting for her turn, Becky Kerkman, the manager and a close friend of ours, walked by and told Chelsea, "You will do great. You have the Holy Spirit in you!" giving her a big hug and a huge smile.

A blessing occurred with this embrace. A tingling sensation from Chelsea consumed Becky. She quickly entered her office, closed the door, and stood in silence and awe. She desired time to absorb and grasp this phenomenon.

"I didn't want this feeling to go away. It seemed to become stronger and more peaceful. It felt like my hair on my head and arms were full of electricity and standing on end. I felt the Holy Spirit so strong from Chelsea."

The Kerkmans were a blessing to our family even before Paul passed away. Becky and I became good friends while Regan and Sydney developed as an extended brother and sister to my children. Our families believed in the same Christian values. We raised our children with similar methods.

Earlier in time, Becky and her husband, Steve, partook in their own spiritual encounter and became blessed with a beautiful baby boy, Matthew Louis.

Jesus said to St. Faustina:

> I thought of you before I called you into being. *"Jesus, in what way were You thinking about me?"* In terms of admitting you to My eternal

happiness. *After these words, my soul was flooded with the love of God. I could not stop marveling at how much God loves us. (1292)*

Matthew became a blessing for our family, much like Regan and Sydney. He continuously filled our lives with unconditional love and smiles, and he aided in filling the deep void we felt every day.

Before Matthew could talk, Becky sometimes showed him pictures of Paul. He always smiled as if he recognized Paul. Becky found this odd. She believes Paul is watching over her son.

I encountered similar incidents. My living room displays a variety of framed family pictures, including a single photograph of Paul. Matthew often approached this picture. He would point at Paul with his tiny finger and smile as if he knew Paul. Other times he picked up the photo and carried it around my house.

I have often heard stories of young children having a special gift of hearing heavenly music, seeing divine visions, or glimpsing of loved ones who have died. I pray Paul *is* watching over our little angel!

Think of what is above, not of what is on earth.

Colossians 3:2

Do not conform yourself to this age but be transformed by the renewal of your mind, that you may discern what is the will of God, what is good and pleasing and perfect.

Romans 12:2

Chapter 38

One Monday afternoon, Zach and I headed for Norfolk. As we approached Tilden, the warning lights on the dash panel began flashing ferociously. The speedometer and R.P.M. gages raced up and down. The car itself drove normal even though it seemed possessed. We weren't going to make our destination before the car ended up stalling, and headed back toward Elgin. Suddenly, all of the lights and gages halted their insane actions.

An inspection of the car showed there were no malfunctions or failures. Together we experienced something profound. We both believe everything has a purpose.

Days later I learned of an accident, a six car pile-up at the exact location, the exact time, and the exact intersection Zach and I would have traveled through when entering Norfolk.

There are no coincidences!

> We know that all things work for good for those who love God, who are called according to his purpose.
>
> Romans 8:28

Chapter 39

One morning, I caught Chelsea sprinting down from her bedroom to the kitchen. She looked petrified. The sound of footprints and creeks from her room's oak floors woke her up. The slight noise appeared beside her bed. She assumed it came from Jake and concealed her eyes from the sunlight of the new day begging her to wake up. With a change of heart and half asleep, Chelsea decided to take a peek at Jake. However, she received an amazing phenomenon. For a split second, a bright light in human form outlined by a brighter glow stood beside her bed, extending its hand and arm toward her. She gasped and blinked. It disappeared.

Both Jake and Zach have seen a black foggy configuration on numerous occasions after Paul died. The figure would be gone in a quick glance back. I was blessed to experience this wonder only once, and I can understand why they were frightened. It got to the point where they wouldn't mention these happenings to me anymore because they didn't want me to think badly of them. I mentioned this black haze to Father Andrews. He wasn't amused or laughing at the situation, but advised us to use holy water.

I attempted to visit church every day. The back pew was my haven at this time. I bore ungodliness and was not worthy to sit close to the tabernacle.

"Come closer to the front," God whispered in my heart. After some time, I acquired enough courage to walk near to the altar. I sat down.

"Father, I miss Paul so much." I began to cry.

"I know, my daughter." The words of love pierced my heart.

Since Paul passed away, all four of us have perceived a buzzing sound accompanied by a vibration sensation. It can be somewhat compared to a large bumblebee. The vibration usually occurred along the bottom of our spine, ribs, or hips. We were never harmed, but merely startled. I assumed I alone dealt with these abnormal matters until the kids mentioned similar events.

Several of us experienced hearing our name spoken in absolute quiet. One time I heard a "Hi!' whispered in my left ear, and turned my head in haste to meet the conversationalist. I saw no one.

With a new sunrise, a voice expressing, "Mom, Mom, Mom!" woke me up. The kids were still asleep in their bedroom.

Another morning I informed Jake and Zach how I sensed their daddy sitting on the edge of my bed the night before. Jake's eyes grew big from fulfillment and satisfaction.

He humbly declared with his dad's grin, "Mom, I prayed dad would be with you last night!"

One evening, Jake heard the floor creak while saying his night prayers. "Don't scare me, Dad, crawl into bed with me," Jake said lifting up his blankets. He truly felt Paul sit on his bed. Delighted with his dad's presence, Jake drifted off to sleep.

> And whatever you ask in my name, I will do, so that the Father may be glorified in the Son. If you ask anything of me in my name, I will do it.
>
> John 14:13-14

> If you remain in me and my words remain in you, ask for whatever you want and it will be done for you.
>
> John 15:7

Chapter 40

Dementia mystifies me. In sharing conversations with my mother-in-law, I am learning the basics. I attempt to sort out reality and what is only tangible in her mind. She grasps her thoughts as authentic. Some days Arlene questions herself on comments she made or on her jumbled memories.

In the sphere of spiritually we need to sometimes believe what we hear and observe even if it seems unfeasible.

Paul's aunt, Josephine Eischeid suffers from dementia. She and her husband, Leo, united in marriage on October 15, 1949. They both resided at their home in Elgin after raising three sons.

One Sunday morning, Chelsea and I arrived at their house to administer Holy Communion to them. Josephine inquired our names. She had no memory of us. In stating who we were, I didn't mention her deceased nephew Paul. Chelsea began the prayer. Josephine interrupted as she pointed and glanced a little above my head and said,

"See that light above your head, that's Paul!"

Again she repeated herself, "That light, see that light above your head, that's Paul!"

As I followed her eyes, she gazed only inches over my head. The ceiling fan and light fixture hung in an area two feet or more from where she stared. Shivers sprinted down my spine. Wide-eyed and speechless, Chels and I turned toward each other. Prayer ceased for the moment. In this twinkling of time, eternity felt so close.

Minutes later, we left their home. My daughter and I slowly and silently closed the front door behind us. In awe of what we just experienced, we exchanged a silent peaceful smile, one of affirmation for we both knew the others thoughts!

"Mom, Josephine wasn't looking at the ceiling fan and light; she looked right above your head!"

"Yeah! It was Daddy!"

> Therefore, I am content with weakness, insults, hardships, persecution, and constraints, for the sake of Christ; for when I am weak, then I am strong.
>
> 2 Corinthians 12-10

Chapter 41

A quiet May evening became bittersweet for our family. Sixth grade graduation for Zach and his classmates was celebrated with a Mass. This solemn occasion seemed to be a small step closer to Zach's maturing and eventually reaching manhood. I didn't want to consider it. I couldn't bear the thought of the additional loss of my kids growing up and leaving me.

Someone was missing. All of the other students seemed blessed with both parents in attendance. Our family sensed an unfilled space in our hearts and in our church pew.

The Mass left me emotional. I faced the challenge to not shed tears for minor personal sacrifices, but instead to concentrate on the continuing *Real Sacrifice* occurring on the altar.

I bit down hard on my bottom lip when tearing up. I didn't want to display any sign of emotions, but my heart slowly splintered into tiny shards. Another anxiety attack began to consume me. Panic and nauseating sensations quickly and quietly developed within me.

What kind of father failed to attend his own son's graduation, even if the celebration simply marked the end of the sixth grade? I mentality foresaw numerous family events Paul would miss: high school graduations, weddings, and grandchildren. I needed to stay strong for Zach.

The last song was sung, and I survived Mass without making a blubbering fool out of myself.

Unknown blessings occurred all around me!

In a discreet manner, I picked up a small downy feather laying on the carpet, thinking, *a feather from Heaven!*

Sisters, Peg Schindler and Sharon Gossman, came rushing up to me.

"Did you see all the feathers? Feathers were falling down from right above you! There was nothing up there! They fell out of nowhere! We were watching them during Mass!" they revealed as they scurried to pick up the remaining feathers.

"Look! There's one! There's another one!" The sisters eagerly picked a number of the small plumages up off the wine-colored carpet.

What just happened? Feathers don't drift down out of nowhere! Maybe we were being blessed from the other side of eternity by things visible and invisible? Instead of fire and brimstone he revealed his love and his blessings with the softness, gentleness, and the humbleness in a cascade of small white feathers.

What an awesome Father!

> Seraphim were stationed above; each of them had six wings: with two they veiled their faces, with two they veiled their feet, and with two they hovered aloft.
>
> Isaiah 6:2

For in him were created all things in heaven and on earth, the visible and the invisible, whether thrones or dominions or principalities or powers; all things were created through him and for him.

Colossians 1:16

Chapter 42

Chelsea, Jake, and Zach stayed at Tintern Retreat Center by Oakdale for a five day J.C. (Jesus Christ) Camp. Chelsea and Jacob were Junior Counselors. It was Zach's first year to experience this yearly retreat for incoming high school freshmen.

At this time in our journey, the farm house was rented to a young married couple. The kids and I moved into my mother-in-law's home in Elgin after an emotional reluctance to purchase the building.

Relocating developed into a miserable summer challenge. Mental and physical sorting as well as discarding possessions strained me. The farm house and several old out buildings contained numerous items through various years and five generations. My responsibility to move my possessions, three kids', Paul's, and an abundance of Arlene's became overwhelming and exhausting. Treasures and family heirlooms squished into our significantly smaller dwelling.

Mourning the deaths of Paul and Jim and dealing with the depression in each of us at different times took its toll. An extended family problem, a facial tumor removed, and appearing in court to be a representative payee for my kids were just the begging of my struggles. Mandatory classes as Power of Attorney for Arlene and dealing with Arlene's "failure to thrive" became other worries. A decision on whether I should keep or sell the farm weighed heavy on my heart. Life centered on ridiculous amounts of paper work which coincided with nursing homes, wills, death certificates, and other legal documents. Playing the role of mom *and dad* was not easy. School absences, homework, and being on constant guard for my hopeless children were demanding. I teetered on the verge of insanity!

This new house lacked intimate memories of our love and the environment of Paul's presence, which we desired to absorb every waking hour. My head advised me to move into town while my heart whispered the opposite. I yearned to stay on the farm. I saw myself being a traitor to Paul and his family.

The three kids lived at the house in town days before I could. They enjoyed all the freedom of being on their own at night, while I remained at the farm. Memoirs and unfinished dreams with Paul might still be physically touchable and maybe, just maybe, would occur.

Life demanded courage and fortitude to loosen my grip on the house. I had to let it go. An assortment of memories of our old life flooded my mind, but I now became required to make new ones. Without Paul it appeared impossible. I didn't want new memories. I wanted to stay in my old ones and in my old life.

The sun departed for the day. I enjoyed our new home and my own little retreat. Snuggled up with a blanket and *The Theology of the Body*, I relished the quietness. I missed the kids, but I knew they were in good hands.

This awesome retreat let the campers be themselves with no peer pressure present. It allowed them to express their personal anxieties and trials and helped them absorb the love and respect for themselves, others, and God.

The evening brought tranquility to the house and neighborhood. No phones ringing or incoming texts, no basketballs bouncing from the outside street or on my living room carpet, and a black television presented complete stillness. I was able to absorb myself in this amazing book once again. Silence.

I am not one who is scared of being by myself. I wasn't alone. I continued to read but repeatedly glanced toward the doorway between the living room and the kitchen. Something didn't feel right.

I got out of my chair and walked over to the doorway. A negative spiritual feeling was near me, lingering and filling my kitchen. I remember Father Andrews telling me several years earlier to always have holy water in the home. A bible verse continuously rang through my mind: *You belong to God, children, and you have conquered them, for the one who is in you is greater than the one who is in the world.*

I applied holy water to my forehead. A sudden chill glided through me and the hair on both of my arms stood straight up. I wasn't scared. I applied more water and in doing so the hair on my neck and the back of my head felt full of electrical energy.

I wasn't afraid even when my brain told me I should be. I knew who was there. He invaded my home one other evening years before when we still lived on the farm. I sprinkled blessed water throughout my home as I contemplated on the earlier bible verse, 1 John 4:4.

A spiritual silence filled the house. He was gone.

> "Therefore do not be afraid of them. Nothing is concealed that will not be revealed, nor secret that will not be known. What I say to you in darkness, speak in the light; what you hear whispered, proclaim on the housetops. And do not be afraid of those who kill the body but cannot kill the soul; rather, be afraid of the one who can destroy both soul and body in Gehenna."
>
> Matthew 10:26-28

Chapter 43

Chelsea enjoyed modeling outfits she purchased in Norfolk earlier that day. While keeping up with the family laundry, I admired my thrifty daughter's taste in style, her teenage modeling, and her maturity.

She paused on one end of the kitchen with me on the other. An upright, empty beverage glass began twirling in a circle on a countertop between us. Neither one of us partook in the movement of this cup. Our wide eyes stared as the glass continued rotating and finally fell to the floor unbroken.

With chills, I sensed an unfriendly visit. Out came the holy water once again!

The night after I consecrated myself to our spiritual mother, Mary, the nightmares began. I was unable to sleep well for days and only remember four of the dreams. Satan knew my weak spots. He concentrated on subjects close the heart and took advantage of my fears.

Paul was "in spirit" in the first dream. However, he conveyed that he was bored of us and wanted to be with someone more exciting. This left me nauseous. *How could Paul do this to us? It's only a dream. It's only a dream!*

My father died repeatedly in the next. I grieved throughout this nightmare and the next day. I was fully aware this delusion wasn't real, yet this deceptive death took a toll on me.

In the third bad dream, I experienced every conceivable sized spider crawling around and on me. I felt their legs, but could not see them. Chelsea picked them up and squished them between her fingers while laughing hideously. I hate spiders!

The fourth vision consisted of large sharp fangs trying to devour me. No matter how much I ran or hid, teeth always found me. I couldn't escape them!

I believed Satan's mission consisted of discouraging me on my commitment to Mary. I shared the events with Becky. She suggested a prayer:

> Prayer To Saint Michael
>
> Saint Michael the Archangel, defend us in battle. Be our protection against the wickedness and snares of the devil. May God rebuke him, we humbly pray; and do Thou, O Prince of the Heavenly Host—by the Divine Power of God—cast into hell, Satan and all the evil spirits, who roam throughout the world seeking the ruin of souls.
>
> Amen.

No unpleasant dreams occurred for me that evening. Instead, Jake ended up having one.

Satan, now you are attacking my most valuable possessions, my children! You're not going to do this!

The next evening before going to sleep, we both prayed to St. Michael for protection from evil. We sprinkled holy water throughout the rooms of our house. It worked!

Thank you God!!

Jesus said to St. Faustina;

> You should not worry too much about adversities. The world is not as powerful as it seems to be; its strength is strictly limited. Know, my daughter, that if your soul is filled with the fire of My pure love, then all difficulties dissipate like fog before the sun's rays and dare not touch the soul. All adversaries are afraid to start a quarrel with such a soul, because they sense that it is stronger than the whole world...(Diary 1643)

> For our struggle is not with flesh and blood but with the principalities, with the powers, with the world rulers of this present darkness, with the evil spirits in the heavens.

Ephesians 6:12

Your Cross

> The everlasting God has in His wisdom foreseen from eternity the cross that He now presents to you as a gift from His inmost heart. This cross He now sends you He has considered with His all-knowing eyes, understood with His divine mind, tested with His wise justice, warmed with loving arms and weighed with His own hands to see that it be not one inch too large and not one ounce too heavy for you. He has blessed it with His holy Name, anointed it with His consolation, taken one last glance at you and your courage, and then sent it to you from heaven, a special greeting from God to you, an alms of the all-merciful love of God.

St. Francis de Sales

Chapter 44

The fourth anniversary of Paul leaving us drew close. I often pondered why life journeys pass us quickly yet travels slowly. How is "time" capable of conveying two different approaches? It felt like Paul departed from our world only an instant ago but seemed like an eternity since I held him last and told him I loved him.

Years before Paul and I ever met, he had a strong desire to become a Catholic priest. Having a family and children held him back from his priestly calling. His deep faith progressed and transformed throughout life's various events. Perhaps his desire began with his ancestral background, originating in a very small cottage in Eischeid, Germany, and for certain, ending his last moments in our home.

As I listen to our living room clock tick minutes away, I comprehend time. Was the latest second utilized for the highest goal, salvation? This moment will never exist again.

I am one of many who are guilty of rejecting God's gift of grace. Our awesome Father incessantly blesses us with more!

How much time do I reflect on the satisfaction of recent family sporting events, the new car sitting n my driveway, or the huge closet overstuffed with possessions? Do my thoughts linger on the big party coming up or achieving a beautiful weed-free lawn?

Or do I reflect on our family's salvation?

Time on earth is only a blink in God's eyes. Eternity is forever. Life's earthly pleasures, success, social standings and material gains become priorities.

"We want the old Karen back," I often heard in a roundabout way from family and friends. That person had dissipated. Chelsea, Jake, Zach, and I are not who we once were. We transformed and grew in our beliefs and values with the experience of countless godsends and trials the past four years. Our family continues to experience these unworldly blessings.

Paul's death was a sincere blessing from God unknown in our hearts and minds at the time. Still today, we feel Paul's physical absence, but we are aware of his spiritual presence, and with each unforeseen life encounter we continue to gently sprout and flourish.

Earlier this morning, Jake, who in the past years was forced to grow up faster than most kids his age, ran with excitement into my bedroom. He was in the basement playing video games. In his heart, he heard the exact same words I understood in my heart four years earlier sitting in church with Paul and our kids.

"Mom, I wasn't even thinking about it! I heard you should write a book and call it,

I Blessed You With Cancer!'"

> Count it all joy, my brothers, when you encounter various trials, for you know that the testing of your faith produces perseverance.
>
> James 1: 2-3